Drugs and the Law

**REPORT OF THE
INDEPENDENT INQUIRY INTO THE MISUSE OF DRUGS ACT 1971**

Chairman: Viscountess Runciman DBE

Drugs and the Law

Report of the
Independent Inquiry into the Misuse of Drugs Act 1971

Report of an independent inquiry established by The Police Foundation, 1 Glyn Street, Vauxhall, London SE11 5RA.

ISBN 0 947692 47 9

Information about this inquiry and information about how to obtain the report are available from:

The Secretary
Independent Inquiry into the Misuse of Drugs Act 1971
1 Glyn Street
Vauxhall
London SE11 5RA

Telephone: 020 7582 3744
Facsimile: 020 7587 0671

Preface

Origin and remit of Inquiry

We were set up in August 1997 by The Police Foundation, with the assistance of the Prince's Trust, to review the effectiveness of the Misuse of Drugs Act 1971. Our report follows. Our membership and terms of reference are set out at Appendices 1 and 2 respectively.

We were assisted in our work by many organisations and individuals and we gratefully acknowledge here our indebtedness to all those who helped and supported us. Further details of this and of our programme of work are given in Appendices 3,4 and 6.

Acknowledgements

We are glad to be able to record our gratitude for the help and support which we have received in the course of this Inquiry. Our greatest debt is to the Trustees, Director and staff of the Police Foundation. They conceived the idea, raised the resources, and ensured our independence. The Foundation's support has been central to our work. We have also benefited from the assistance which we have received from the Prince's Trust, especially during the Inquiry's early stages.

Several Trusts made grants towards the Inquiry's work. They were the Peacock Trust, Esmée Fairbairn Charitable Trust, Minerva plc, The Joseph Rowntree Foundation, The Prince's Trust, The Pilgrim Trust, The Hayward Trust, The Wates Foundation and The Tompkins Foundation. The substantial financial help which we received from them underpinned the entire Inquiry and enabled us to commission research and seek evidence which would not otherwise have been available to us and which played an important part in informing our decisions.

At most of our meetings we were privileged to be able to discuss the many complex issues involved with some of the foremost experts and professionals in their field. We list them at Appendix 3. We were also greatly helped by those individuals and organisations who responded to our request for written evidence. They are listed at Appendix 4.

We held meetings with three groups of young people in different parts of London. Our thanks go those who facilitated our discussions with them, which were very illuminating and instructive. We have not named the young people we met or the organisations which enabled us to do so.

We owe much to the Home Office Research, Development and Statistics Directorate, who provided us with data additional to the published statistics which placed extra demands on them in their already demanding timetable. The Home Office Action Against Drugs Unit enabled us to attend a seminar on drugs issues addressed by Professor Mark Kleiman of the University of California at Los Angeles. They also responded unfailingly to our many requests for information. We appreciate the sanction given to this work by both Permanent Under Secretaries of State during the period of our Inquiry.

We are also much indebted to the Netherlands Ministry of Health, Welfare and Sport whose representative, Mr. A. D. J. Keizer, answered innumerable queries as well as coming over to discuss Dutch policy with us together with a colleague, Mr. Ed Leuw, from the Netherlands Ministry of Justice. We are very grateful to them both.

We have kept in touch informally with the progress of the working party on Drug Misuse and Public Policy set up by the Royal College of Psychiatrists and the Royal College of Physicians, who also arranged a joint seminar addressed by Professor Peter Reuter of the University of Maryland. We greatly appreciated the cooperation of the working party and the Chairman, Dr.Robert Kendell.

The Institute for the Study of Drug Dependence (ISDD) conducted a study for us of the legal position in six European Union member states, France, Germany, Italy, the Netherlands, Spain and Sweden. The resulting report, edited by Nicholas Dorn and Alison Jamieson, brings together and synthesises contributions from six national legal experts from the countries concerned. It has proved invaluable in enabling us to understand other countries' approaches to the same problems that we face and to appreciate the differing ways in which it is possible to implement the international conventions that apply to all of them. We are most grateful to the editors and the national experts for producing it.

We were able to survey the attitudes of schoolchildren and adults to drugs through two surveys conducted on our behalf by Market and Opinion Research International (MORI). We discuss the main findings in Chapter Two of our report. We gladly record the unfailing assistance of MORI's researchers in this enterprise, which covered ground that had not been explored before.

We asked Professor Howard Parker of Manchester University to produce for us a submission explaining, on the basis of published and some unpublished research, how young people make decisions about whether or not to try or use one or more of the illicit drugs. His submission has proved an essential introduction to this crucial topic.

Professor Michael Levi of Cardiff University prepared for us an overview of financial measures such as confiscation of assets and legislation against money laundering. This was enormously helpful for our understanding of a notoriously complex area.

Professor Robert Baldwin prepared an instructive note for us on the regulatory alternatives to the criminal law in dealing with drugs.

We have held 28 meetings and are grateful to the Law Society for providing the facilities for these. British Airways organised and supported the travel of one of our members between the United Kingdom and the United States for many months. We greatly appreciate their generosity. We are also grateful to the British Airports Authority for letting us use their management centre at Pease Pottage near Crawley for a special two-day meeting.

We have been most fortunate in our Secretariat. William Saulsbury, our Secretary, organised and directed our work with unfailing efficiency, tenacity and good humour. Joy Mott, our Research Secretary, brought long experience of research in drugs and the criminal justice system, and guided us through the labyrinth of statistical and research material. James Addison, former Secretary to the Royal Commission on Criminal Justice, minuted our meetings and drafted much of the report with skill and speed which has our united admiration. We owe a great deal to Sue Roberts who cheerfully and efficiently dealt with a very heavy administrative burden.

The advice and support of Colin Phillips, representing the Prince's Trust, has been of great benefit to us.

Without this array of help and support our work would not have been possible. We are very grateful for all of it. The results are our responsibility alone.

Contents

Tables

Figures

Overview

1   It is nearly 30 years since the main legislation controlling the misuse of drugs in the United Kingdom was enacted. Our task has been to consider the changes which have taken place in our society in that time and to assess whether the law as it currently stands needs to be revised in order to make it both more effective and more responsive to those changes. It has also been our duty to examine the implications of our proposals.

2   In the course of our Inquiry it has become inescapably clear to us that the eradication of drug use is not achievable and is not therefore either a realistic or a sensible goal of public policy. The main aim of the law must be to control and limit the demand for and the supply of illicit drugs in order to minimise the serious individual and social harms caused by their use. At the same time, the law must enable the United Kingdom to fulfil its international obligations.

3   The law should be based on the following principles and purposes:
  (i)   as a means of reducing demand, the law is only one aspect of a broader agenda of health, prevention and education. It should not undermine other elements of that agenda – indeed, it should be able to support them;
  (ii)   it should reflect the latest scientific understanding and the social and cultural attitudes of modern British society;
  (iii)   it should be realistically enforceable;
  (iv)   it should infringe personal freedom only to the degree necessary to restrain serious levels of harm to users or others;
  (v)   it should target the drugs that cause the most harm;
  (vi)   it should reflect the relative harmfulness of activities connected with each illicit drug or category of drugs, and provide for sanctions proportionate to that harm;
  (vii)   in its operation, the law should be accepted by the public as fair, consistent, enforceable, flexible and just. The proper exercise of discretion may be an important means of achieving this.

4   Throughout our Inquiry we have been forcibly struck by the lack of research and the weakness of the information base about drug use in the United Kingdom, including the lack of any 'early warning systems' to identify and monitor significant changes in drug use such as have been developed in the USA and the Netherlands. Equally striking is the anomaly that the largest part of the drugs budget is spent on enforcement without the necessary resources being applied to the proper evaluation of its success or failure. We welcome the new research programme of the latest national plan, but until it begins to yield significant results and embraces some of the issues raised in this Report, discussion of the policy options will continue to be hampered by the need for more research and better evaluations than we have at present. Nevertheless, whatever its deficiencies, such evidence as we have assembled about the current situation and the changes that have taken place in the last 30 years all point to the conclusion that the deterrent effect of the

law has been very limited. We have sought to assess effectiveness by the standard indicators of prevalence, public attitudes, and by trends in the availability, price and purity of controlled drugs.

5   In this report we use the terms 'problem' and 'casual' drug use in their now commonly accepted senses. By 'problem drug use' we mean use whose features include dependence, regular excessive use and serious health and other social consequences; it will typically involve the use of opiates, particularly heroin, cocaine or other stimulants, often as part of a pattern of polydrug use. We use 'casual' in its dictionary definition of 'not regular or permanent or calculable, varying with circumstances'. In distinguishing between problem and casual drug use, we do not imply that the latter is problem free or does not involve a variety of risks. We only consider that objective terminology is required to distinguish between those with serious drug problems and others who use drugs.

6   Taking the standard indicators in turn, the evidence shows that there has been a significant increase in the prevalence of both problem and casual drug use in the United Kingdom over the past 30 years. Although the data is poor, the trend of a substantial and steady increase in problem drug use is clear, producing estimates of up to 200,000 problem drug users of whom the majority are heroin users, often injectors. The largest increase in problem drug use over the last 5 years has been among those under 21. There is a high correlation with social deprivation and urban residence, but more recently there has been a wider social and geographical dispersal together with significant local variations. There has also been a large increase in this period in the numbers of casual drug users, especially of those who use cannabis. One of the features of casual drug use in the last decade has been the very substantial increase in the numbers of young people using a wide combination of drugs, particularly stimulants, in leisure settings.

7   We would emphasise that, although prevalence is often taken as the prime indicator of the drugs problem and the measure of success in controlling it, prevalence studies are largely estimating the number of occasional users, particularly of cannabis, who cause little harm either to themselves or to others; a much smaller number of heroin users inflict much greater harm on themselves and on others. The consequences of drug use are more important than the numbers of users.

8   The evidence that we have collected on public attitudes shows that the public sees the health-related dangers of drugs as much more of a deterrent to use than their illegality, the fear of being caught and punished, availability, or price. There are also significant differences in public attitudes to cannabis compared to other drugs.

9   Despite large increases in the number and quantity of seizures of all drugs, there is no strong evidence that drugs have become harder to obtain or more expensive. Nor has there been any decrease in purity. There has also been a growth in the range of synthetic drugs available.

10   All the evidence suggests to us that the law plays a minor part in deterring demand. It is of prime importance, therefore, that the law should accurately reflect relative harm in terms of current knowledge and experience. Only then can it support a public health agenda of education and prevention.

11   The law is and must remain the principal means through which supply is curtailed. But we see no evidence that severe custodial penalties are deterring traffickers, or that enforcement, however vigorous, is having a significant effect on supply. The Misuse of Drugs Act 1971 was framed at a time before drugs had become the chief commodity of organised crime. We have come to the conclusion that the law and, more particularly, its implementation, need strengthening to make it more difficult both to derive huge profits from drug trafficking and to reinvest those profits in the drug trade and other criminal enterprises for further gain.

12   In considering possible changes to the law in the light of this evidence, we have been very conscious that the Misuse of Drugs Act 1971 reflects a long historical process of international agreements on drug control in which the United Kingdom has been a major participant. As such, one of its objectives is to implement this country's obligations under the three current international conventions. We have found a widespread belief that these obligations rule out the possibility of changes to the law. In fact, although they rule out the legalisation of any prohibited drug other than for medical, scientific or limited industrial purposes, the conventions allow more room for manoeuvre than is generally understood. All our recommendations fall within the requirements of this country's international commitments.

13   It is in the area of drug use, possession and related acts that the scope left by the international conventions for different approaches is widest. We have found that it is not well understood that for such offences there is express provision for imposing measures such as treatment, education, rehabilitation or social reintegration. These measures may be imposed either in addition or, more importantly, as an alternative to conviction or punishment.

14   The study conducted for us of other European countries' drug laws shows that use can be, and is being, made of this room for manoeuvre. It shows that while there is close harmonisation in response to trafficking offences, there is considerable divergence of approach towards drug use and possession and towards acts of minor supply. We have concluded that there are some useful European lessons for the United Kingdom.

15   We have found that the United Kingdom has a more severe regime of control over possession offences than most of the other European countries which we have studied. Although direct comparisons are difficult because of incompatibilities as well as deficiencies in both the quality and quantity of the data, we have seen no evidence which would warrant the conclusion that the United Kingdom has benefited from the more punitive provisions of its law on possession.

16   The United Kingdom is unique in Europe in having a three-tier classification system by which the law ranks drugs according to their relative harmfulness and attaches penalties to the class in which a drug is placed. We have concluded that this classification is useful and should be retained. It enables the relative risks of different drugs to be more accurately distinguished in terms of current scientific and sociological knowledge. It also allows sanctions to be applied which are proportionate to the harms of the drugs and the activities related to them.

17   However, the criteria by which drugs are classified have never been clearly described. We believe that they should be. We have undertaken this exercise as best we could within the time, resources, and expertise available to us, and we hope it will be built upon. It has led us to conclude that some drugs should be reclassified so that the classes provide a more accurate hierarchy of harm and commensurate sanctions. We recommend the following transfers between classes:

(i)   cannabis from B to C (a recommendation first made in 1979 by the Advisory Council on the Misuse of Drugs);

(ii)   cannabinol and its derivatives from A to C;

(iii)   ecstasy from A to B (a recommendation made to us by the Association of Chief Police Officers among others);

(iv)   LSD from A to B;

(v)   buprenorphine from C to B.

18   We recognise that some of these changes may be thought to risk conveying potentially dangerous messages to drug users and prospective users. We believe, on the contrary, that the changes will enable the law to reflect more accurately the risks attached to different drugs. This will enhance the law's credibility and the support it can offer to education and prevention. We have concluded that the most dangerous message of all is the message that all drugs are equally dangerous. When young people know from their own experience that part of the message is either exaggerated or untrue, there is a serious risk that they will discount all of the rest. Recent evidence indicates that there is a pressing need to refocus education and attention on the pre-eminent harm of heroin and cocaine.

19   We next considered the offences stipulated and defined by the law. We see the need to strengthen the law's armoury against supply by creating a new offence of dealing which would allow the courts to sentence for a course of conduct rather than only for an isolated act of supply. We also found a need for change in the offences relating to premises, paraphernalia, the cultivation of cannabis and the regulations relating to the therapeutic use of cannabis. In each case our aim has been to enhance the law's capacity to reduce harm where those who use drugs are concerned, and to concentrate in line with the national strategy on those who produce, process, distribute and sell them.

20   With regard to all trafficking offences, we believe that much would be gained by statutory sentencing guidelines and we hope that the new Sentencing Advisory Panel will so advise the Court of Appeal. Such guidelines should incorporate the aggravating factors to which we believe the courts should have consistent regard in their sentencing. Key aggravating factors which should be included are: the involvement of an organised criminal group; the use of violence or firearms; the use of children or young persons in trafficking activities; supply to minors; the commission of the offence in the vicinity of schools, psychiatric facilities or prisons; and public nuisance elements in the offence.

21   We have concluded that the most serious deficiency in the law against drug trafficking is a pragmatic rather than a legislative one. It lies in the current ineffectiveness of the procedures by which the assets of drug traffickers are

confiscated under the Drug Trafficking Offences Act 1994. The facts speak for themselves: in 1997, the total amount ordered to be confiscated was £5.6 million, a fifth of the amount confiscated in 1994, while the average order of £3,800 was the lowest ever. We see a need to transfer responsibility for enforcing confiscation orders from the magistrates to the crown court; also for the establishment of a National Confiscation Agency, as recently proposed by the Home Office, tasked with ensuring that the confiscation process achieves full efficiency. We stress, however, that if this is to be achieved, considerable investment is needed in recruiting and training people with the requisite skills. These will be needed in most branches of the criminal justice system, in particular the police, prosecution and courts (including the judges). We believe that a radical shift to civil confiscation should not be considered before the ability of the current criminal system to function more effectively has been fully developed with the aid of these proposals.

22   Possession offences dominate the operation of the law against drugs. They constitute around 90% of the total of MDA offences and they take up a very large amount of the time and resources of the criminal justice system. After careful consideration of the evidence presented to us on the operation of the law, here and elsewhere, we have concluded that imprisonment is neither a proportionate response to the vast majority of possession offences nor an effective response where the offence is related to problem drug use. A prison sentence should be abolished as a penalty for most possession offences.

23   There is one, and only one, respect in which we believe that the power to impose a custodial penalty should be retained. We have in mind those cases of possession of a Class A drug where the harm represented by the offence is such that the courts must have available to them powers currently dependent on a liability to imprisonment. These include the powers to impose certain community sentences with a full range of sanctions for breach. We have accordingly recommended that there should be no custodial penalty for the possession of Class B and C drugs, but that a shorter maximum prison sentence than at present should continue to be available for the possession of a Class A drug.

24   Our recommendation is already accepted, at least tacitly, by the courts. Although the maximum prison sentences for possession under United Kingdom law, from 2 to 7 years, are among the severest in Europe, they are not, in fact, imposed. Current sentences for possession are very much shorter at an average of less than 4 months and the evidence suggests that it is unlikely that many of the 4,852 people given custodial sentences for possession offences in 1997 were in prison for the offence of possession alone. Under our recommendations, we would expect prison sentences for possession to be rare, and imposed only where community and treatment sentences had failed or been rejected.

25   The law's viability where possession offences are involved has depended on the massive increase in the use of cautioning by the police. It is now used in over half of all such cases. We think the police have been right in their approach, but we consider that discretion needs a proper framework within which to operate. Like

the Royal Commission on Criminal Justice in England and Wales, we think that cautioning should become a statutory sanction, with guidelines set down in regulations. This would bring with it the important option for conditions attached to a caution to be enforced, which is not possible at present. Recently the Government has published proposals to bring cautions, along with reprimands and warnings, within the ambit of the Rehabilitation of Offenders Act 1974 and to make them immediately spent for the purposes of the duty of disclosure by the offender in most cases. We welcome this proposal. We would go further and we recommend that a caution, like a fiscal fine in Scotland, should not bring with it a criminal record. Regulations should spell out where and how a caution is to be recorded and disclosed to answer the needs of the police and of the courts. Either way, it has clearly become necessary for cautioning itself to become a statutory procedure.

26   We fully support the national strategy's aim to protect communities from drug-related crime: the violence of turf wars; the degradation of neighbourhoods from drug markets; and the crimes linked to problem drug use. We recognize that the courts need to have available a wide range of powers to tackle the link between drugs and crime. In the case of drug users, our view that prison sentences should be abolished for most possession offences will not interfere with those powers. Those offenders for whom such powers are appropriate will almost invariably be charged with acquisitive offences whether or not they are also before the courts for possession offences. It is important to remember that even though their cost to society is great due to the scale of their offending, it is a minority of problem drug users who commit crime and they are not usually involved in serious or violent crime but rather in small scale acquisitive crime, particularly shoplifting.

27   We are aware that a practical consequence of our recommendations would be to deprive the police of their power of arrest for a possession offence which comes to light following a stop and search. Currently Class A or B possession offences are arrestable offences by virtue of the fact that they attract a prison sentence of 5 years or more. We agree with the police that the objectives of the law as we have defined them would be undermined if this power was abolished. We wish to see the power of arrest continue to apply, as at present, to the possession of Class A and B but not Class C drugs.

28   The major change which would follow, therefore, from our recommendation that cannabis should be reclassified as a Class C drug is that the power of arrest would no longer apply to offences of possession of cannabis, except in certain prescribed circumstances such as when an offender's identity is in doubt. Cannabis possession offences are by far the largest category of all drugs offences – 78,000 out of a total of 113,000 in 1997. The police have argued to us that this could reduce their operational effectiveness against the drug problem across a broader front. Their fear is that they would be hampered in their ability to disrupt local markets and to obtain intelligence about suppliers. They also point out that they would be deprived of the consequential PACE power to search the premises of those arrested, which may bring to light Class A drugs and weapons. The evidence we have seen does not, however, persuade us that more would be lost than gained

by the removal of the police power of arrest for cannabis possession. We think that the power to stop and search for drugs which we accept must be retained, together with arrest powers for Class A and B drugs, will be enough to ensure that intelligence-led and street-level policing is not undermined.

29   It will be apparent that our recommendations about cannabis are those that would bring about the greatest change. That is our intention. While we have encountered no sense that the legislation on drugs overall needs radical change, we have encountered much unease and scepticism about the law and its operation in relation to cannabis. Cannabis is not a harmless drug: there are physical and psychological risks to the individual from regular, long-term cannabis use, and there are dangers to others from the impairment to motor and cognitive functioning from intoxication. But by any of the main criteria of harm – mortality, morbidity, toxicity, addictiveness, and relationship with crime – it is less harmful to the individual and society than any of the other major illicit drugs, or than alcohol and tobacco.

30   Our conclusion is that the present law on cannabis produces more harm than it prevents. It is very expensive of the time and resources of the criminal justice system and especially of the police. It inevitably bears more heavily on young people in the streets of inner cities, who are also more likely to be from minority ethnic communities, and as such is inimical to police-community relations. It criminalises large numbers of otherwise law-abiding, mainly young, people to the detriment of their futures. It has become a proxy for the control of public order; and it inhibits accurate education about the relative risks of different drugs including the risks of cannabis itself. Weighing these costs against the harms of cannabis, we are convinced that a better balance is needed and would be achieved if our recommendations were implemented.

31   Under our proposals, the normal sanctions for offences of cannabis possession and cultivation for personal use would be out-of-court disposals, including informal warnings, statutory cautions or a fixed fine on the model of the Scottish fiscal fine. Prosecution would be the exception, and only then would a conviction result in a criminal record. We recognise that if the sanctions for cannabis possession and cultivation, both in the law and its enforcement, were to be substantially reduced there would be a risk that more people would use it. But the international evidence does not suggest that this is inevitable or even likely. Given the current widespread availability and use of cannabis, we judge that more would be gained in terms of credibility, respect for the law and the police, and accurate education messages than would be lost in potential damage to public and individual health by the control regime which we recommend. We also believe that our proposed regime would promote the targeting of enforcement on those drugs and activities which cause the greatest harm, in line with the objectives of the national strategy. It would also accord with public perceptions of where policing priorities should lie.

32   In our consideration of cannabis, we have looked carefully at the Dutch experience and taken evidence from both proponents and opponents of their present policy. The Dutch are widely and wrongly believed to have legalised cannabis. While

cannabis remains explicitly illegal, Dutch policy has, in effect, created a regulated market for the small-scale supply of cannabis to adults through coffee shops. This approach has not been without its problems or contradictions. Nevertheless, we have been impressed by its results. These indicate: a similar level of cannabis use to other countries; a lower prevalence than in the United Kingdom, especially among young people aged 16 – 19; a stable population of problem drug users, with a rising average age, and a high proportion of them in touch with treatment services; virtually no volatile substance misuse, and a ratio of drug-related deaths which is the lowest in Europe. We think that there are two important lessons for the United Kingdom. The first is the potential benefit of treating demand problems as primarily health problems, with the result that the social exclusion of young people through drug offending is kept to a minimum. The second is the potential benefit of separating the market for cannabis from that for heroin in particular.

33 We believe that there is much that is instructive in the approach of other European countries besides Holland, and that we should be constantly alive to the lessons of their experience. We have been interested, for example, in the administrative and civil sanctions of Italy and Spain, the distinction between private and public offences in several countries, the different definitions and approaches to acts of group supply, and policies of non-prosecution which, in some German *Länder* for instance, currently operate in 80 - 90% of offences of personal possession of cannabis.

34 Nor should we forget the lessons of our own experience. There is one respect in which the United Kingdom has scored a significant success in the interests of public and individual health. The strategy to curb the spread of HIV among injecting drug users involved abandoning moral absolutes in favour of harm reduction together with a huge effort to expand services and to attract problem drug users to them. The overall result has been a steady decline in HIV prevalence among drug injectors throughout the 1990s including significant decreases in areas of high prevalence in Scotland. Today prevalence in the United Kingdom is lower than in any other Western European country of similar size. That strategy needs to be maintained and reinforced, and the law and its implementation used to support it, as in the development of needle exchanges.

35 Our overall conclusion is that demand will only be significantly reduced by education and treatment, not by the deterrent effect of the law. What is needed is a less punitive approach to possession offences at the same time as a more effectively punitive approach to supply. We see no inconsistency in this. If the harm caused by drugs is to be significantly reduced, long custodial sentences for supply are clearly not a sufficient deterrent. It must be made much more difficult for traffickers to profit from supplying drugs and for those who have profited to escape confiscation and forfeiture. But harm will not be reduced by disproportionate penalties and criminal records for many, mainly young, people whose largely occasional drug use could more effectively be tackled by earlier and more credible education about the nature and degree of risk, especially long-term risk. Nor will harm be reduced by imprisoning those whose problematic drug use could more effectively be helped by treatment and rehabilitation in a setting where

all the other problems almost always associated with such drug use can be tackled too. It is clear to us that tackling problem drug use must always also involve tackling social deprivation.

36 We have also considered the issue of the therapeutic use of cannabis. We are in no doubt that the therapeutic benefits of cannabis use by people with certain serious illnesses outweigh any potential harm to themselves or others. We have nothing to add to the detail of the Report of the House of Lords Select Committee on Science and Technology. We are particularly surprised that one of the grounds for the Government's summary rejection of its recommendations should be anxiety about the capacity of GPs to withstand pressure for the prescription of cannabis when they have always been able to prescribe heroin for pain without any apparent problem. We do not consider that the relevant International Convention prevents the transfer of cannabis and cannabis resin from Schedule 1 to 2 of the Regulations, thereby allowing its prescription. We recognise that until the current research programme produces a cannabis plant with a standard dose of THC, the main psychoactive ingredient, rules will need to be devised to govern what is to be provided under prescription, and by whom. We do not see that as an insurmountable problem. In the interim, we have recommended a specific defence in the law in the event that a person is charged with possessing, cultivating or supplying cannabis for the relief of certain medical conditions.

37 Over the last two decades there has been growing evidence from research showing that treatment is effective in reducing drug use and the criminal activity related to it and that it is cost effective. The Government's 10-Year Strategy places a strong emphasis on the role of the criminal justice system in directing problem drug users into treatment. We accept the rationale for using the criminal justice system in general, and the law in particular, as a route to treatment. At the same time, however, all our evidence points to a serious shortage of treatment services in the United Kingdom. There needs to be a substantial reallocation of resources from enforcement, which currently takes up 62% of the total drugs budget, to treatment services, which receive 13%. There also needs to be much greater investment in evaluating treatment approaches.

38 The national strategy recognises the shortfall between treatment capacity and demand and has plans to tackle it. But in the short to medium term we believe that the shortage will continue and the ability of the criminal justice system to act as a conduit to treatment will therefore be limited, haphazard, and potentially unjust. It is important that treatment via the criminal justice system should be carefully targeted, should not distort the use of services and the allocation of resources and should not be used to replace other routes to help. The fact that research on arrest referral schemes shows that a large proportion of those arrested were not in touch with services is an argument for more services not for more arrests.

39 It is not widely understood that the Misuse of Drugs Act 1971 is also the instrument whereby the provision and use of controlled drugs for legitimate medical purposes is regulated. The evidence presented to us suggests that more

effective monitoring and control of excesses in the system is required. There has been an increase in deaths from overdose, particularly of methadone, together with continuing leakage of prescribed controlled drugs onto the illicit market. There is evidence that private prescribing tends to be for larger quantities, particularly of injectable drugs, at higher doses, and for longer periods. We think there is a case for the licensing of private prescribing of Class A drugs to problem drug users based on training, experience and links to specialist services. The prescribing regulations need to be amended to enable all controlled drugs to be prescribed in instalments in England and Wales as is the case in Scotland. At the same time, there are several small but significant changes which should be made to the regulations to aid pharmacists who face many difficulties in their important role in relation to problem drug users.

40 Drug laws in all countries reflect the tension between cultural history and changing attitudes and practice. They also reflect the tension between the rights and freedoms of the individual and a public desire to use state action to limit harms to individuals and communities. Our aim in reforming the present law has been twofold: to reduce the harm that drugs can do to individuals and to reduce the harm to which we believe the present law is leading. We believe that our changes would advance both these aims. They would produce a law which is less intrusive, less detrimental to the individual and more enforceable. They would also produce a law that is more effective in targeting the most dangerous drugs and related activities.

41 Any law must win the consent of the majority in a democracy. A change in the law can move only as far as that consent is maintained. Attitudes to drugs, across all age groups, have shifted and will continue to shift. We believe we are moving with the grain of that consent, especially with regard to cannabis. Our proposed changes are legally sound, and reflect priorities already observed by those most closely involved in the implementation of our drug legislation. They also bring the law into line with public opinion and its most loyal ally, common sense.

Chapter One: The Legislation in Context

Introduction

1   The main instrument for drugs control in the United Kingdom is the Misuse of Drugs Act 1971 (the MDA). This needs to be seen in the context of other Acts of Parliament and the United Nations conventions on drugs. We start with the United Nations conventions because the MDA is the means by which the United Kingdom seeks to meet its international obligations as a signatory to those conventions, although its scope extends beyond the conventions.

2   The United Nations conventions require the states that are party to them to meet certain broad obligations, including the creation of criminal offences. But the conventions leave considerable leeway as to how precisely those obligations are to be met in the domestic law of the country concerned. This is not widely understood and we therefore commissioned the Institute for the Study of Drug Dependence (ISDD) to undertake a programme of comparative legal research into the national drug laws of France, Germany, Italy, Spain, the Netherlands and Sweden. We believe that this study[1] is a very useful contribution to public understanding of the international context, and we draw on it throughout this report. It illustrates in particular how all countries party to the conventions broadly converge in their laws against trafficking in illicit drugs but take a variety of approaches to possession for personal use. All such variations can be interpreted as allowable within the provisions of the conventions, although there has been some debate as to whether certain countries are fully convention compliant.

3   Although often thought of as purely prohibitory, both the MDA and the conventions recognise that most if not all illicit drugs have or have had valuable and legitimate medical, scientific and industrial uses. As well as prohibiting the use of the drugs concerned outside these lawful fields, the conventions and the MDA (mainly through the regulations made under section 7) are concerned to ensure that their use within these areas continues to be possible. They are thus flexible regulatory instruments under which much remains permitted. They should not be regarded as solely repressive.

4   The relationship between our domestic law and international agreements is not a recent one. It goes back at least as far as 1920, when the Dangerous Drugs Act was passed in order to enable the United Kingdom to ratify the Hague Convention of 1912 (preceded by the Shanghai Commission of 1909). This set the pattern for United Kingdom legislation to emerge from international agreements, although it has always been possible for the United Kingdom, as for other countries, to take action in advance of or separately from international conventions. Normally, however, the international conventions have indicated the minimum that needs to be done, individual countries being left to do more if they wish. The general pattern can be seen in the summary of the main events in the history of drugs control in the United Kingdom, which we set out in Appendix 5.

---

[1] *Room for Manoeuvre: Full Report,* April 1999, unpublished.

The United Nations conventions

5   There are three United Nations conventions on international cooperation in the drugs field. They date from 1961 (with a protocol added in 1972), 1971 and 1988. The 1961 convention consolidated and replaced the earlier treaties and conventions that were relevant, which is why it is entitled the 'Single Convention on Narcotic Drugs 1961'.

6   The Single Convention does not in fact define the term 'narcotic' and some of the substances identified in the Schedules to the convention may not fit comfortably with the description. Its aim is continuous international cooperation and control in order to limit such drugs to medical and scientific purposes. There are also exceptions for industrial purposes; for example the convention does not prohibit the cultivation of the cannabis plant exclusively for industrial or horticultural purposes. The drugs are arranged in schedules which determine the level of control applied to a given drug. The controls include limitations on manufacture, production, cultivation, importation and possession as well as requirements of labelling, keeping records, prescribing and safe custody. Activities that are contrary to the convention are to be 'punishable offences when committed intentionally' and punishment is to include imprisonment in serious cases. Although the convention does not specifically require that states create criminal offences, it is difficult to see how countries such as the United Kingdom could create punishable offences in any other way. Countries with different legal traditions, and especially those with differently developed forms of administrative law, may be in a different position.

7   The Convention on Psychotropic Drugs 1971 is, as its title implies, concerned with psychotropic drugs, but the term 'psychotropic' is not defined in the convention. The substances concerned, which include hallucinogens, stimulants and sedatives, are listed in four schedules which determine the restrictions to be applied. The aim of the 1971 convention, as of the Single Convention, is to limit the use of drugs to medical or scientific purposes. Schedule 1 lists substances whose use is to be prohibited 'except for scientific and very limited medical purposes by duly authorised persons, in medical or scientific establishments which are directly under the control of their Governments or specifically approved by them'[2]. The very restrictive wording of the convention when it comes to the drugs in this schedule prevents their being made available on prescription, and explains why the drugs listed, which include some cannabis-type substances such as cannabinol (except for dronabinol), are not in normal medical use in the United Kingdom. By contrast cannabis and cannabis resin are narcotics controlled by the Single Convention. As with the 1961 convention, actions contrary to the convention must be treated as punishable offences and be liable to adequate punishment including imprisonment.

8   Commentaries have been published by the United Nations interpreting various provisions of the conventions. These commentaries reveal that the references to possession, purchase and cultivation may not have been intended to cover possession, purchase or cultivation for personal use. This seems to have been

---

[2]Article 7 (a)

regarded as a loophole which on most interpretations was closed by the 1988 convention.

9   The United Nations Convention against Illicit Traffic in Narcotic Drugs and Psychotropic Substances 1988 (The Vienna Convention) supplements and strengthens the earlier conventions. It specifies that breaches of the conventions should be established as *criminal* offences under each state's domestic law. At the same time the activities that are to be designated as criminal offences are clarified and extended. Trafficking in particular is defined in great detail so as to include all possible forms of organisation, management and financing of illicit drugs activity. New controls are introduced over chemicals (usually referred to as precursors) which have legitimate uses but can also be used to manufacture illicit drugs. Parties are required to create new offences of money laundering as well as to adopt measures to strip traffickers of the proceeds of their trade.

10   The 1988 convention also requires that each party establishes as a criminal offence the possession, purchase, or cultivation of illicit drugs for personal consumption[3]. This closes the loophole mentioned above[4]. There is, however, a distinction between the penalties for trafficking and those for personal consumption offences. Trafficking offences must be liable to sanctions which take into account the grave nature of such offences. The sanctions should include imprisonment or other forms of deprivation of liberty, pecuniary sanctions and confiscation[5]. There is no similar requirement to have imprisonment, pecuniary sanctions and confiscation available as penalties for personal consumption offences[6].

11   The conventions leave precise implementation of many matters to individual states. For example, in the 1988 convention it is stated that nothing shall affect the principle that the offences concerned shall be defined, prosecuted and punished in conformity with the domestic law of a party. There are similar reservations in the earlier conventions. In the 1961 and 1971 conventions the obligation to create punishable offences is subject to a country's 'constitutional limitations'. In the 1988 convention this becomes 'subject to [a country's] constitutional principles and the basic concepts of its legal system'. But in the 1988 convention the saving clause applies only to the criminal offences of possession, purchase or cultivation for personal consumption. Where the possession, purchase or cultivation is for trafficking, and with respect to trafficking offences generally, the requirement to establish criminal offences is absolute and may not be evaded on grounds of being contrary to a country's constitutional principles or the basic concepts of its legal system. The effect is to allow far more room for manoeuvre for personal consumption offences than for trafficking offences.

12   These factors allow significant variation across states in such matters as the drafting of offences, the classification of drugs, maximum penalties and actual sentences. The references to constitutional limitations or principles are significant chiefly for those countries where the use or possession of illicit drugs is not a criminal offence because the constitution is interpreted as giving individuals the right to harm themselves. The reservation that prosecution is to be in conformity with domestic law provides parties to the conventions with a high degree of latitude not to

---

[3]Article 3, paragraph 2
[4]See paragraph 8
[5]Article 3, paragraph 4(a)
[6]Article 3, paragaph 4 (d)

prosecute offenders (or to divert offenders from the criminal justice system) when it is appropriate in the public interest to do so. This again most commonly happens in the case of use or possession for personal use. The conventions permit parties to adopt measures that may be more strict than those provided by the conventions if, in their opinion, such measures are desirable or necessary for the protection of public health and welfare.

13   All three conventions are concerned with prevention and treatment as well as with punishment. The 1961 convention requires the parties to 'give special attention to and take all practicable measures for the prevention of abuse of drugs and for the early identification, treatment, education, after-care, rehabilitation and social reintegration of the persons involved...'. It provides also that 'when abusers of drugs have committed...offences, the Parties may provide, either as an alternative to conviction or punishment or in addition to conviction or punishment, that such abusers shall undergo measures of treatment, education, after-care, rehabilitation and social reintegration...'. Much the same approach and wording appears in the 1971 convention.

14   This approach is refined in the 1988 convention. The scope for using measures of treatment, education, aftercare, rehabilitation or social integration as alternatives or in addition to punishment varies with the offence involved. For serious trafficking offences they may only be provided in addition to conviction or punishment[7]. For offences of personal consumption, on the other hand, they may be applied either as alternatives or in addition to conviction or punishment[8]. But there is a grey area: in appropriate trafficking cases of a minor nature the non-punitive responses may be used as an alternative to conviction or punishment[9]. This is therefore another area where states have some flexibility in deciding on the appropriate response to drugs offences.

Other countries' approaches

15   In order to give some idea of the room for manoeuvre permitted under the United Nations conventions, we give below some examples[10] of how the law in other European countries differs from our own. Our purpose is merely to illustrate the scope given by the conventions for variations of approach. As may be seen, some countries use administrative law rather than criminal law to respond to drug use or possession for use. It must, however, be noted that it does not follow that the intensity of administrative enforcement measures is any less strict or severe than measures enforced in the United Kingdom (even though enforcement in the United Kingdom is usually by means of the criminal justice system). For the purposes of the European Convention on Human Rights and the Human Rights Act 1998 a measure may be treated as being penal (and thus a criminal law measure) even if it is described as being administrative or civil in nature. If so it attracts the same requirements for procedural safeguards (due process, rights of appeal and so on).

16   Major trafficking. Other European countries distinguish in various ways between minor and major forms of trafficking. All the countries in the ISDD study provide

---

[7]Article 3, paragraph 4(b)
[8]Article 3, paragraph 4(d)
[9]Article 3, paragraph 4(c)
[10]Most of these are taken from the report cited at footnote 1.

for special penalties if the offence is committed by a manager or member of a group engaged in organised crime. Spain and Italy identify in their law aggravating factors that include being a person in authority, supplying to minors, using minors to commit a drugs offence, and introducing drugs into schools, prisons or social welfare centres.

17 <u>Minor supply.</u> In Italy it is not a criminal offence to share drugs without payment among a group of users. In Spain the setting up of a common fund by a number of addicts for the purpose of acquiring drugs for consumption among themselves has been declared not a matter for prosecution. Administrative sanctions may, however, apply (in Spain only if the sharing takes place in public). In the United Kingdom and other countries the person who passes drugs round within a group would be treated as a supplier even if he is a member of the group.

18 <u>Cultivation</u> of cannabis is an administrative not a criminal offence in Spain if the drug is intended for personal use. In Spanish law there is no difference of treatment as between cultivation and other acts intended to obtain drugs for one's own use.

19 <u>Possession.</u> In Spain possession for personal use is not a criminal offence but a serious administrative offence, although one that is unlikely to be punished unless committed in public. Italy also treats possession for personal use as an administrative rather than a criminal offence. Administrative penalties can be quite punitive, involving for example fines or loss of driving licence, gun licence or passport.

20 <u>Use.</u> Italy, the Netherlands and Germany do not prohibit drug use in the sense of personal consumption. Spain applies administrative sanctions when use is in public. In Sweden and France use is a criminal offence. In the United Kingdom it is an offence to use opium under section 9 of the Misuse of Drugs Act 1971 (MDA) but otherwise the relevant offence is possession, as in other countries which do not specifically make use an offence.

21 <u>Discretion.</u> In the Netherlands there is a formal written policy providing guidelines for the investigation of offences under the Opium Act, first issued in 1976 and most recently revised in 1996. Under these the normal practice is to take no action against possession of small quantities of any drug for personal use. This is in accordance with the expediency principle permitting minor cases not to be prosecuted in the public interest. The same principle is applied to the sale of small amounts of cannabis (5 grams and under) from coffee shops, though it is less clear whether it applies to the sale of stocks (up to 500 grams) to those coffee shops and their cultivation or importation. In Germany discretion varies between the extremes of non-intervention in some Länder in cases of possession for personal use, and rigorous enforcement in others.

The Misuse of Drugs Act 1971

22 The Misuse of Drugs Act 1971 replaced the Drugs (Prevention of Misuse) Act 1964 and the Dangerous Drugs Acts of 1965 and 1967. It thus brought all

controlled drugs under the same statutory framework. In doing so, it also incorporated: the relatively new system of licensing doctors to prescribe heroin and cocaine[11] to addicts; the requirement for all doctors to notify addicts to the Home Office; regulations on the safe custody of drugs; and national stop and search powers for the police. It also established the first statutory advisory body, the Advisory Council on the Misuse of Drugs. The Act's system of classification was also new. Drugs were placed in three Classes, listed in Schedule 2 to the Act, and penalties for offences were related to the Class of drug involved in the offence. The offence of unlawful possession was divided between possession and possession with intent to supply, and a new defence was provided for people claiming lack of knowledge of the essential ingredients of certain drugs offences.

23   Section 1 establishes an Advisory Council on the Misuse of Drugs whose duty it is to keep the drug situation in the United Kingdom under review and to advise government ministers on the measures to be taken for preventing the misuse of drugs or for dealing with the social problems connected with their misuse.

24   Section 2 identifies the drugs to be controlled. They are listed in a schedule that is divided into three parts and are called 'Class A', 'Class B' or 'Class C' drugs depending on the part in which they appear. Confusingly the drugs are sometimes described as being Schedule 1, 2, 3, 4 or 5 drugs: such references are not to the Classes in Schedule 2 to the Act but to the Schedules to the related Misuse of Drugs Regulations 1985[12]. The significance of the Classes is that, where a criminal offence is committed, the maximum penalties are determined by the Class of drug involved in the offence.

25   Sections 3 to 6 set out the main activities which, unless there is an exemption in the regulations made under section 7, are criminal offences if a controlled drug is involved. Under section 3 importation and exportation are prohibited although the actual offences are contained in and prosecuted under another statute, the Customs and Excise Management Act 1979. The other main offences covered are production, supply, possession, and possession with intent to supply. The cultivation of the cannabis plant is a separate offence under section 6 but it is also production under section 4. This is because the definition of 'cannabis' in section 37 of the MDA was widened by section 52 of the Criminal Law Act 1977 so that it included virtually the whole plant and not just the flowering and fruiting tops. The courts have subsequently held that production of cannabis is equated with its cultivation[13].

26   Section 8 makes it an offence for the occupier or someone concerned in the management of premises knowingly to permit or suffer those premises to be used for (a) the production or (b) the supply of any controlled drug, (c) the preparation of opium for smoking or (d) smoking cannabis, cannabis resin or prepared opium. Section 9 prohibits smoking or otherwise using opium; frequenting a place used for smoking opium; and possessing utensils for smoking or preparing it. Section 9A makes it an offence to supply or offer to supply any article (except a hypodermic syringe) which the supplier believes may be used or adapted to be used in the unlawful administration (including self-administration) of drugs. The exemption

---

[11] The licensing requirement was extended to dipipanone in 1985.
[12] See paragraphs 27 and 28 below
[13] *Taylor v. Chief Constable of Kent* [1981] 1 W.L.R. 606

for hypodermic syringes was made as part of the national strategy to curb the spread of HIV through injecting drug use. Further offences are created in sections 18 to 21, including incitement to commit any offence under the MDA (section 19) and, while in the United Kingdom, assisting in or inducing the commission of offences in any place outside the United Kingdom (section 20 – the offence has to be one punishable under a corresponding law in the other country).

27   The regulations made under section 7 ensure that the appropriate exemptions are made from the offence provisions of the Act. Most controlled drugs have many legitimate medical or scientific uses. Their day-to-day use for medicine or for scientific research would not be possible if the doctors, pharmacists and scientists concerned were to be regarded as committing criminal offences in the course of their work. The regulations therefore ensure that legitimate activities are exempted from the relevant offence provisions of the MDA. What the Act prohibits, the regulations allow[14].

28   There are also controlled drugs, and preparations and products containing controlled drugs, which do not need to be subject to the full force of the MDA. For example schedule 5 lists certain products which may be freely imported or possessed despite containing controlled drugs (some of them in Class A) in minute quantities. Benzodiazepines are Class C drugs but, with the exception of temazepam since 1996, they are excepted from the prohibition on importation, exportation and, when in the form of a medicinal product, possession. Anabolic steroids are not subject to any prohibition on possession when in the form of a medicinal product, but can only be imported or exported in such a form by a person for administration to himself. These results are achieved by placing the substances concerned in the appropriate schedule or part of schedule to the regulations. We explain the difference between the schedules to the regulations in Chapter Three. The significance of the schedules is quite different from that of the Classes in the Act, to which they bear no relationship. We emphasise this because we found that the position was widely misunderstood.

29   Section 10 gives wide powers to the Secretary of State to make regulations governing safe custody, documentation of transactions, record keeping, packaging and labelling, transport, methods of destruction, prescriptions, the supply of information on prescriptions to a central authority, the licensing of doctors to supply controlled drugs to addicted patients, and the notification by doctors of their addicted patients. The Addicts Index set up under the last power has been abolished, but the power under section 10(h) still exists and could in theory be used in future. Under section 11 the Secretary of State may give notice to the occupier of any premises on which controlled drugs are kept of precautions that must be taken for the safe custody of those drugs. It is an offence to contravene any directions given.

30   Sections 12 to 16 enable the Secretary of State to withdraw, by direction, the authority of a doctor, dentist, veterinary surgeon, veterinary practitioner, or pharmacist to prescribe, administer, manufacture or supply specified controlled drugs. There are procedures for referring cases at various stages to tribunals, advisory bodies or panels as appropriate.

[14]See Chapter Three, paragraphs 42-45.

31   Section 23 gives the police powers to search premises and to stop and search persons on suspicion that they are in possession of a controlled drug. Powers of arrest are set out in section 24, which is still valid in Scotland but has been replaced in England and Wales by sections 24 and 25 of the Police and Criminal Evidence Act 1984. We explain these powers more fully in our discussion of possession offences[15].

32   Maximum penalties are provided for in sections 25 and 26 and forfeiture of anything relating to the offence in section 27. Importation, production, supply, possession with intent to supply and section 20 offences are defined as trafficking offences for the purposes of the Drug Trafficking Act 1994. So is incitement, if it is incitement to commit a trafficking offence. Under the Crime (Sentences) Act 1997 a third consecutive trafficking offence involving a Class A drug attracts a mandatory minimum sentence of seven years imprisonment.

33   Most MDA offences (including production, supply, possession with intent to supply, possession, cultivation of cannabis and offences relating to opium under section 9) are subject to the provisions of section 28. This section enables a defendant to prove a lack of knowledge of facts relevant to a charge. A defendant cannot be acquitted if he believed the drug was controlled yet erred as to the precise nature of it. On the other hand he will be acquitted if he neither believed, nor suspected, nor had reason to suspect that the substance was a controlled drug at all. Where the prosecutor has to prove some other fact relevant to the charge, it is open to the defendant to prove that he neither knew, nor suspected, nor had reason to suspect the existence of it. Without section 28 the offences to which it applies would be absolute (i.e. the defendant could be convicted without proof of any guilty knowledge). It is nevertheless a high hurdle for a defendant to overcome compared to provisions which require the prosecution to prove knowledge, as is the case with importation offences under the Customs and Excise Management Act 1979 and premises offences under section 8 of the MDA.

Related legislation

The Customs and Excise Management Act 1979

34   The interrelationship between the MDA and the Customs and Excise Management Act 1979 (hereafter CEMA) is complex. Section 3 of the MDA prohibits the importation or exportation of any controlled drug unless (i) there is an exception allowing importation or exportation in regulations made under section 7 or (ii) the importation or exportation takes place under licence issued by the Secretary of State. It is not, however, the MDA that makes it an offence to contravene this prohibition. Instead the relevant offences are set out in CEMA. It should be noted that regulations made under the MDA, or a licence issued by the Secretary of State under the MDA, may have the effect of preventing a particular action from being an offence under CEMA.

---

[15]Chapter Five, paragraphs 20-23

Table 1.1 Maximum penalties for main drug offences

Offence	Mode of Trial	Class A	Class B	Class C
Importation[1] Production Supply Possession with Intent to supply	Summary £5,000 or both	Six months or a fine of £5,000 or both	Six months or a fine of £2,500 or both	Three months or a fine of
	On indictment or both	Life or an unlimited fine or both	14 years or an unlimited fine or both	5 years or an unliminted
Section 20[2]	Summary			Six months or a fine of £5,000 or both
	On indictment			14 years or an unliminted fine or both
Possession	Summary	Six months or a fine of £5,000 or both	Three months or a fine of £2,500 or both	Three months or a fine of £1,000 or both
	On indictment	Seven years or an unlimited fine or both	Five years or an unlimited fine or both	Two years or an unlimited fine or both
Cultivation of cannabis plant[3]	Summary	Six months or a fine of £5,000 or both	Six months or a fine of £5,000 or both	
	On indictment	14 years or an unlimited fine or both	14 years or an unlimited fine or both	
Premises offences[4]	Summary	Six months or a fine of £5,000 or both	Six months or a fine of £5,000 or both	Three months or a fine of £2,500 or both
	On indictment	14 years or an unlimited fine or both	14 years or an unlimited fine or both	Five years or an unlimited fine or both
Offences relating to opium[5]	Summary	6 months or a fine of £5,000 or both		
	On indictment	14 years or an unlimited fine or both		
Paraphernalia[6]				Six months or a fine of £5,000 or both[7]
Incitement	The maximum penalties are the same as for the offence incited.			

Notes: [1]Under the Customs and Excise Management Act (CEMA). [2]Assisting in or inducing the commission outside the United Kingdom of an offence punishable under a corresponding law in force in that place. The Class of drug is not relevant. [3]Section 6. [4]Section 8. [5]Section 9. [6]Section 9A. [7]The maximum penalties are the same irrespective of the mode of trial. The Class of drug is not relevant.

The Medicines Act 1968

35   The Medicines Act 1968 is a wide-ranging statute that regulates the many activities associated with the production and distribution of medicinal products, particularly when any of those activities are carried on commercially. 'Medicinal product' is a term which is defined broadly and includes many substances that may not usually be regarded as being medicinal at all. Many require marketing authorisation or a licence before they may be distributed in the course of business. Complex and detailed provisions are made in the Act and its many regulations for the testing, sale, supply, packaging, labelling, prescribing, dispensing by pharmacists and selling in shops of medicinal products. The Act enforces this administrative regime with statutory criminal offences. Many controlled drugs are also medicinal products or the ingredients of such products. Thus substances that are supplied often attract the provisions of both the MDA and the Medicines Act, as well as their associated regulations, and prescription requirements in particular may arise under both enactments.

The Criminal Justice (International Co-operation) Act 1990

36   Part II of the Criminal Justice (International Co-operation) Act 1990 was passed to enable the United Kingdom to comply with the Vienna convention of 1988[16]. It lists a number of chemicals (often termed precursors) that can be used to manufacture illicit drugs. These are subject to various controls designed to minimise the risk of their being obtained by criminals. Manufacture or supply contrary to section 12 is a trafficking offence for the purposes of the Drug Trafficking Act 1994. Notification of export, record keeping and the supply of information are required by regulations made under section 13. It is an offence to fail to comply with the regulations or to furnish false information in an attempt to comply with them.

The Drug Trafficking Act 1994

37   The Drug Trafficking Act 1994 is largely a consolidation of earlier legislation. It enables the United Kingdom to meet its obligations under the 1988 convention, in particular to create offences in connection with the laundering and handling of the proceeds of drug trafficking and to introduce measures to confiscate those proceeds. The convention allows the burden of proof to be placed on the accused to prove that the assets were lawfully acquired. The Act implements this and applies the civil standard of proof on the balance of probabilities, rather than the criminal standard of beyond reasonable doubt. It also designates which offences are to be treated as trafficking offences[17]. We describe the provisions of this important legislation, and our proposals for extending it, in greater detail in Chapter Four.

---

[16]See paragraph 9
[17]See paragraph 32

Chapter Two: The Present Situation

Introduction

1   It is nearly 30 years since the Misuse of Drugs Act was introduced. The purpose of this chapter is to describe the present situation and the main changes that have taken place in these three decades. The chapter reviews what is known about the scale and nature of drug use in the United Kingdom. It reviews the drug seizure and offender statistics, in terms of the numbers of drug offenders and how they are dealt with. Finally, it presents important new evidence from a survey specially commissioned by the Inquiry which explores public attitudes towards drugs in today's Britain.

2   A major change has been the steady increase in problem drug use. In the late 1960s there had certainly been a sharp increase in heroin use and addiction which had prompted various government enquiries prior to the 1971 Act. Even so, the difficulty was almost entirely confined to certain sections of London and involved not many more than 1,000 known addicts. By the mid 1980s there had been a significant increase in both the scale and geographical spread of problem drug use, and that trend has continued to the present.

3   An important feature of the last two decades has been the growth in injecting among problem drug users, particularly of heroin and amphetamines. This has given rise to major public and individual health problems, in particular HIV and more recently hepatitis C. From the mid-80s the HIV-risks of injecting drug use have given grounds for serious concern. The risks of an epidemic were starkly illustrated in Edinburgh where by 1988 the prevalence of HIV among injecting drug users was reported to be as high as 50%. A national strategy of harm reduction measures to curb the spread of HIV through injecting drug use was adopted and energetically pursued. A key component of the strategy was an increase in services, including needle exchanges and substitute prescribing.

4   There was a substantial fall in the proportion of problem drug users injecting, from 65% to 47% between 1989 and 1996. Currently HIV prevalence among injecting drug users in the United Kingdom is lower than in any other Western European country of similar size. However, the continuing increase in problem drug use and the current evidence of a slight growth in the proportion of those who inject underlines the need to sustain and increase such interventions. High levels of hepatitis C among problem drug users are a new and perplexing challenge.

5   Since the 1970s, and at an accelerating pace during the 1980s and 1990s, increasingly large numbers of people have been prosecuted under the MDA. The vast proportion of these have been for the simple possession of controlled drugs, particularly cannabis, rather than for offences of importation, production and supply. Since the 1980s there has also been a growing concern about drug-related crime, not just drug offences themselves, but acquisitive crimes such as burglary, shoplifting and robbery as well as violence surrounding the control of drug

markets. These crimes have a grave impact both on the community and on the criminal justice system.

6   On some estimates, as much as one-third of all property crime in the United Kingdom is reckoned to be drug-related – particularly to heroin and cocaine. Pilot studies which test for drug use among people arrested for a variety of offences show that in some areas between one-fifth and one-third tested positive for opiates, and one-quarter tested positive for cocaine[1]. These consequences of problem drug use were simply unknown thirty years ago.

7   An equally striking change is that a much larger section of the population is familiar with the more commonly used illicit drugs, such as cannabis and amphetamines. The majority of people do not use illicit drugs and, of those who do, most do not do so regularly and frequently. Nevertheless, familiarity and experimentation with drugs has become much more commonplace, involving important changes in attitudes and experience.

8   Well past the 1960s illicit drug use remained a minority pursuit. By the late 1990s surveys consistently show that a majority of young people between 16 and 29 years admit to having tried illicit drugs. As many as one-quarter to one-third of this group might have used cannabis and other drugs on a casual basis within the last year or last month.

9   A major cultural shift in attitudes to drugs and their use has occurred in the United Kingdom over the past 30 years. Social attitudes towards drug use have become more nuanced and sophisticated, not only among the young. The survey conducted for us by MORI shows that among adults aged 16 – 59 twice as many as not regard cannabis as less harmful than alcohol – but the great majority do regard heroin, cocaine, ecstasy and tobacco as particularly harmful. Perhaps surprisingly in terms of common stereotypes, there is no evidence of a generation gap in these matters. If anything, more people aged 45-59 years saw cannabis as less harmful than alcohol than did those aged 16-24.

10   Taken together, the changes in the scale of drug-related problems, much wider familiarity with some forms of illicit drug use, and social attitudes which no longer lump all drugs together, provide the context for our examination of current illicit drug use and efforts at its control.

Scale and nature of drug use

11   A picture of drug misuse and the law's response can only be put together by looking at information from several sources. These include the Home Office statistics of people notified by doctors as addicts, the Department of Health statistics from the regional drug misuse databases of people who begin attending drug treatment services, and information from national and regional surveys of self-reported drug use. The annual Home Office Statistics of Drugs Seizures and Offenders Dealt With is also an important information source. Several of these sources have significant limitations, which we note at the appropriate points. Often this means that the figures from some sources must be regarded as indications of trends rather than actual numbers.

---

[1] T. Bennett, *Drugs and Crime: the results of research on drug testing and interviewing arrestees*, Home Office Research Study 183, London, Home Office, 1998.

The Addicts Index

12   From 1968 until April 1997 doctors had a statutory duty to notify the Home
Office of patients who, in their judgement, were addicted to one or more of a
number of Class A drugs, including cocaine, heroin and methadone. The annual
statistics of this Addicts' Index identified separately the number of addicts who had
been notified for the first time and those who had been notified previously. But the
numbers were serious understatements of the true position because many addicts
did not seek treatment, and many of those who did were not notified by their
doctors.

13   Between 1973 and 1996 the total number of new and renotified addicts increased
by over 1000%, from 3,022 to 43,372, with the number of new addicts increasing
by 2000%. Between 1974 and 1996 the number of notified heroin addicts
increased by almost 2000% (from 607 to 15,271). Local studies over the years
have led to general agreement that the real number of addicts was between two
and five times the number notified, the true figure in the mid-to-late 1990s was
probably between 100,000 and 250,000 addicts in the UK.

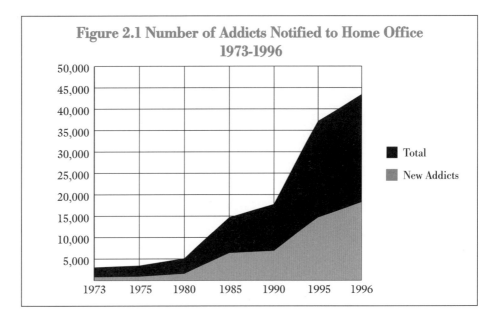

The regional drug misuse databases

14   Since 1993 the Department of Health has published six-monthly statistics of
problem drug users. These are figures of people reported by drug treatment
agencies to regional drug misuse databases in Great Britain as beginning
attendance at a treatment agency or returning after a break of six months or more.
However, the information is seriously defective. There is no legal requirement for
treatment agencies to report, and those who seek treatment for the first time are
not separately identified. There is no certainty that all problem drug users who
attend agencies are included in the databases or that there is no double counting
between agencies. Because of the time lag in their production, the statistics cannot
provide early warning of new local outbreaks of problem drug use. Since, however,
doctors are no longer required to notify their addict patients, these statistics now

provide the best available indicators of the extent, pattern and nature of heroin and other problem drug use in Great Britain.

15   What the regional drug misuse databases appear to tell us is that between 1993 and 1998 the number of people seeking help increased from approximately 20,000 to 35,000. In this same period, males consistently outnumbered females by 3 to 1. Slightly more than one-half were aged 20 to 29 years, with roughly one in six aged 19 years or younger. The remainder, slightly less than one-third, were aged 30 years or more. The proportion saying heroin was their main drug of misuse rose from 43% to 56%.

National and regional surveys

16   There is no systematic national survey evidence of self-reported drug use for the period to compare with the Addicts Index and its evidence of steady increases in heroin addiction and other forms of problem drug use since the early 1980s. This is because surveys of this kind are largely a phenomenon of the 1990s.

17   Such surveys have their critics who point to their unreliability: sample sizes vary, and are generally too small to measure meaningful changes; despite reassurances of confidentiality, respondents may conceal or exaggerate their drug taking, or they may be less willing to admit to the use of more stigmatised drugs such as heroin and cocaine. Furthermore, surveys tend to ask 'Have you ever used a drug?' which is not a sound indicator of current behaviour. The important issues are whether people are using drugs regularly, and if so how often and how recently.

18   All these are reasonable objections, and certainly such surveys are unlikely to capture highly problematic drug users with chaotic lifestyles, homeless, or in institutions. Even so, such surveys show a great deal of consistency and tell us something about current patterns of drug use in the United Kingdom.

19   The first survey in England and Wales to inquire about the use of particular drugs was in 1969[2], and offers a broad brush-stroke comparison with the 1990s. Four per cent of respondents (aged 16-69 years) said that they had used amphetamine at some point in their lives, 2 per cent had used cannabis, and less than half a per cent mentioned the use of any other drugs. Comparable figures from the 1998 British Crime Survey (BCS) of people aged 16-59 years are 32 per cent saying that they had ever used any drug, including 10 per cent saying that they had ever used amphetamine, and 25 per cent saying that they had ever used cannabis.

20   The 1994, 1996 and 1998 BCS[3] all found that around twice as many people admit to having ever taken drugs as admit to taking them in the last year. This suggests that much drug use is experimental, although people may be more willing to say they have taken drugs on an occasional basis a long time ago.

21   If we look only at those who admit that they had taken drugs in the last year or month, better indicators of regular use, we find little change between 1994 and 1998 as the figures below show.

---

[2]P. Marks et al, *Public attitudes to drug taking: short report on work carried out through the OPCS for the Home Office*, unpublished 1973.
[3]M. Ramsay and A. Percy, *Drug Misuse Declared: results of the 1994 British Crime Survey*, Home Office Research Study No.161, London, Home Office 1996.
M. Ramsay and J. Spiller, *Drug Misuse Declared in 1996: latest results from the British Crime Survey*, Home Office Research Study No.172, London, Home Office 1997.
M. Ramsay and S. Partridge, *Drug Misuse Declared in 1998: results from the British Crime Survey*, Home Office Research Study No.197, London, Home Office 1999.

Table 2.1   British Crime Surveys: people who said they had taken any drug last year and last month. Percentages of age groups.

Aged:	16 to 59	16 to 29
1994		
Last year	10	23
Last month	6	14
1996		
Last year	10	24
Last month	6	15
1998		
Last year	11	25
Last month	6	16

22   Cannabis is by far the drug most likely to have been used either *last year* or in the *last month*. Using the 1998 BCS figures it is estimated that almost two and a half million 16-29 year olds in England and Wales had taken cannabis *last year*, and one and a half million had done so *last month* – that is, almost one-third of the sample said they had used it in the *last year* and one in five in the *last month*. Half of those who admitted taking any drug *last year* said they had used cannabis only. The other half had used cannabis as well as other drugs, or other drugs only.

23   BCS data regularly show that only a very small percentage – one per cent or less – admit to using heroin or crack cocaine. There is some indication of an increase of powder cocaine use during the 1990s, although among younger people amphetamine remains by far the most popular drug after cannabis. The 1998 BCS reports 5% of 16-29 year olds saying that they used it in the *last month*, and 8% in the *last year*.

24   16 to 19 year olds are the age group most likely to say they take 'hallucinants' (amphetamines, ecstasy, LSD, magic mushrooms and amyl nitrite). The proportion in this age group taking any of these drugs in the *last year* dropped between the 1994 and 1998 BCS from 18% to 12%.

25   The findings of the 1993 and 1996 Scottish Crime Surveys[4] are broadly similar to those of the BCS, with cannabis the drug of choice. The Northern Ireland Crime Survey[5] of 1994/95 indicates far lower levels of drug use, with only 5 % of the total sample admitting to the use of cannabis, again the most popular drug by far. A recent study of ecstasy use in Northern Ireland[6] does point to pockets of much higher levels of illicit drug use – reflecting the wide regional variations in levels of use evident elsewhere in the United Kingdom.

26   The only regularly collected information on drug use by 11 to 15 year-old schoolchildren comes from the annual surveys on health behaviours carried out by the Schools Health Education Unit[7]. These surveys are useful although not nationally representative. The surveys from 1990 to 1997 found that one in ten of

[4]S. Anderson and M. Frischer, *Drug Misuse in Scotland: findings from the 1993 and 1996 Scottish Crime Surveys,* Research Findings No.17, Edinburgh, The Scottish Office Central Research Unit 1997.
[5]*Experience of drugs in Northern Ireland: preliminary findings from the 1994/5 Northern Ireland Crime Survey,* Research and Statistics Branch Research Findings 1/96, Belfast, Northern Ireland Office 1996.
[6]K. McElrath and K. McEvoy, *Ecstasy Use in Northern Ireland,* London, The Stationery Office 1999.
[7]J. Balding, *Young People in 1998,* Exeter, Schools Health Education Unit 1999.

the 11-13 year-olds sampled said that they had *ever taken* drugs. Of the 14-15 year-olds, a third said that they had *ever taken* drugs in 1995 and 1996; this fell to a quarter in 1997 and 1998. The nationally representative 1998 figures from the Office of National Statistics show the first downturn in the number of schoolchildren ever having used a drug[8]. At the other end of the educational spectrum, a national survey of second year university students in 1995[9] found that 20% said that they were regular (i.e. at least once a week) cannabis users. 4% said that they used amphetamines regularly and 3% ecstasy. Less than one per cent said that they used any other drug.

27   The heaviest drug users and those with serious problems are unlikely to be found by household or school surveys. A new source of trends in high-risk groups is provided by those surveys of people held in police custody for a variety of offences. These combine voluntary and confidential urine testing of arrestees with interviews on drug use. This is a method used in the United States for more than ten years. In a pilot study begun in 1996/97, a sample of arrestees in five police areas in England agreed to provide urine samples for drug testing[10]. The urine tests showed that 61% had taken at least one drug. Cannabis was the drug most likely to be found. It occurred in the tests of 54% of the 16 to 20 year-olds, 47% of those aged 21 to 30, and 37% of those aged 31 and older. The 21 to 30 year-olds were most likely to test positive for opiates (26%), cocaine (14%), amphetamine (14%) and benzodiazepines (15%). These proportions are very much higher than those found for the most comparable age groups in the 1998 BCS. There were also some sharp regional variations.

European comparisons

28   International comparisons are difficult to make because different countries use different survey methods, track different drugs and define age groups differently. The European Monitoring Centre for Drugs and Drug Addiction (EMCDDA) brings together the available information in their annual reports on the state of the drugs problem in the European Union. Unfortunately they have been unable to establish true comparability in the face of the national variations in collecting statistics.

29   There are, however, some comparable figures for the proportions of young adults taking drugs in the last year. See Table 2.2, below. The figures derive from surveys conducted in 1995 or 1996[11]. Although care must be taken in drawing inferences from this information as the age ranges are dissimilar, they do offer some indication of comparative use between countries.

---

[8]Office of National Statistics, *Smoking, Drinking and Drug Use Among Young Teenagers in 1998,* Volumes 1 and 2, London, The Stationery Office 1999.
[9]E. Webb, C. Ashton, P. Kelly and F. Kamali, 'Alcohol and drug use in UK university students', *The Lancet,* 346 (1996), 922-925.
[10]Report cited at footnote 1.
[11]European Monitoring Centre for Drugs and Drug Addiction, *Annual Report on the state of the drugs problem in the European Union 1998,* Luxembourg, Office for Official Publications of the European Commission 1998. Table 2.

Table 2.2   **Last 12 months' prevalence of drug use in recent nationwide surveys among the general population in some EU countries**

Country	Age range	Cannabis	Cocaine	Amphetamines	Ecstasy
Belgium (Flanders)	18 - 39	2.7%	0.5%	0.7%	0.5%
Germany (former West)	18 - 39	8.8%	1.6%	1.5%	1.6%
Spain	15 - 39	11.6%	3.2%	1.7%	2.2%
France	18 - 39	8.9%	0.3%	0.6%	—
Finland	16 - 34	5.2%	—	—	—
Sweden	15 - 34	1%[1]	—	—	—
United Kingdom	16 - 29	21%	1%	8%	4%

Note 1. All illegal drugs

30   Surveys of schoolchildren aged 15 or 16 were carried out in most EU countries between 1995 and 1997[12]. These surveys asked respondents if they had *ever taken* drugs. The highest proportions of those who had used cannabis, over 30%, were found in the United Kingdom, Ireland and the Netherlands. The lowest, less than 10%, in Luxembourg, Finland, Sweden and Portugal. The United Kingdom also had the highest proportion who had used solvents, amphetamines and LSD, and with Ireland and the Netherlands it had the highest proportions who had used ecstasy.

Drug-related deaths

31   Deaths resulting from the use of controlled drugs are obviously a matter of social importance, and also attract a great deal of publicity when they occur. Regrettably, the available public information on drug-related deaths – mainly coroners' statistics – are notoriously difficult to interpret, since coroners might not always know or record whether controlled drugs are involved. Nor do figures record deaths from conditions associated with injecting drug misuse. A working group of the Advisory Council on the Misuse of Drugs has been examining the whole subject of drug-related deaths, including the collection of more reliable and complete statistics, and will report during 2000.

32   In the meantime, it is only possible to say that recorded drug-related deaths have undoubtedly risen since the early 1980s, and that these are mainly resulting from the use of heroin, methadone and other opiates. In England and Wales recorded deaths associated with drug dependence, non-dependent abuse, or poisoning by controlled drugs rose from about 1,800 to 2,100 between 1979 and 1997[13].

[12]In the report cited in the previous footnote, Table 3.
[13]Office of National Statistics Mortality Statistics.

Seizures, prices and purity of controlled drugs

33   The purpose of seizures of drugs together with related law enforcement activity is to disrupt the illicit drugs market. To see whether this has been successful, we looked for evidence of a decrease in the availability of drugs, increases in prices, and reductions in purity.

34   The number, type and quantity of seizures varies from year to year with the resources and activities of the enforcement agencies as well as the traffickers. In 1997, the number of seizures of controlled drugs by HM Customs and the police, at 139,174, was the highest ever recorded, and over twice the 1990 number.

35   The number of heroin seizures more than doubled between 1990 and 1995, and almost doubled again to over 12,000 in 1997. The quantity seized almost quadrupled to 2,200 kgs. in 1997. Between 1990 and 1997 the number of seizures of powdered and crack cocaine rose from 1,805 to 5,432, with the quantity seized quadrupling to 2,350 kgs. There were also increases both in the number of seizures and in the quantities seized of amphetamines and cannabis. However, there were fewer seizures of LSD, and smaller quantities of this substance seized. After the dramatic increase in the number of seizures of ecstasy-type drugs between 1990 and 1996, rising from 399 to 6,211 (with the number of doses seized increasing from 44,000 to almost six million) there was a drop to 5,087 seizures in 1997 (with two million doses seized).

36   Cannabis accounted for much the largest number of seizures and quantity of any drug seized. It was involved in 87% of seizures in 1990 and 77% in 1997, with the weight seized increasing nearly fivefold to150,000kg. The number of cannabis plants seized increased from 34,299 to 114,988, virtually all seized by the police.

37   A report by the National Audit Office[14] noted that the street prices of most types of drugs have shown a flat or falling trend over the period 1990 to 1997/98. Information supplied by Europol suggested that in April 1998 the street price of many drugs was higher in the United Kingdom than in Germany and the Netherlands.

38   Average purities of drug seizures analysed by the Forensic Science Service show fluctuations. The average purities of police seizures of heroin between 1990 and 1997 showed, with small annual fluctuations, that purity decreased slightly between 1990 and 1997. During the same period the purity of cocaine had increased.

39   The 1999 EMCDDA annual report on the state of the drugs problem in the European Union[15] says that cannabis prices appear to be stable. On heroin it says 'The general impression is of price stability after a decrease in previous years' except in Italy where the price is believed to have risen. Much the same report is given for cocaine, with the addition that 'the overall picture is of an expanding market with increased availability'. Prices are said to have decreased for amphetamines and ecstasy.

40   In summary, we found little evidence to indicate that enforcement efforts have led to increased prices, decreased availability or decreased purity.

[14]House of Commons Committee of Public Accounts, Fifteenth Report, *HM Customs and Excise: The Prevention of Drug Smuggling*, London, The Stationery Office 1999. Paragraph 30 and Figure 5.
[15]European Monitoring Centre for Drugs and Drug Addiction, *Annual Report on the state of the drugs problem in the European Union 1999*, Luxembourg, Office for Official Publications of the European Commission 1999. Page 23.

Drug offenders

41   People arrested for offences may be dealt with in a variety of ways. They may be prosecuted or, in England and Wales and Northern Ireland but not in Scotland, the police may formally caution them. In Scotland procurator fiscals have two options for dealing with offenders in lieu of prosecution. They can issue written warnings and may make a conditional offer of a fixed penalty known as a fiscal fine. Under the Customs and Excise Management Act 1979 (CEMA), H.M. Customs and Excise may offer compounding (the payment of a monetary sum in lieu of prosecution) to people attempting to import small quantities (10 grams or less) of cannabis. The police or prosecuting authority may, as an alternative to any of these responses, decide to take no further action. Such cases do not appear in the criminal statistics.

42   Since 1974, the first full year of operation of the Misuse of Drugs Act 1971, the number of offenders against the MDA found guilty, cautioned, given a fiscal fine or dealt with by compounding has risen steadily from 11,811 to 111,384 in 1997, an almost tenfold increase. If offenders against related legislation (mainly CEMA) are taken into account, the scale of the increase is similar since 1974, from 12,532 to 113,154.

43   The great majority of persons dealt with for drug offences are dealt with for possession offences (89% in both 1974 and 1997). In contrast only 16% of drugs offenders dealt with in 1997 were found guilty or cautioned for trafficking offences (defined in the Drug Offences Act 1994 as including importation, production, supply and possession with intent to supply). It should be noted that production figures since 1995 include cases of cultivation of cannabis.

44   Cannabis dominates possession offences, and cannabis possession dominates all offences against the MDA. Since the early 1970s over three-quarters of all possession offences have consistently involved cannabis. Cannabis possession has accounted for between 70% and 85% of all offences against the MDA.

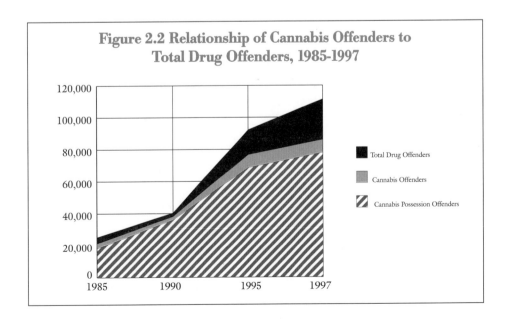

45   If the vast majority of offenders are dealt with for offences involving cannabis, amphetamine is next most frequently involved, 12% in 1974 and 1997; followed by heroin, 4% in 1974 and 8% in 1997; and cocaine, 3% in 1974 and 1997. In 1990 1% were dealt with for offences involving ecstasy, and 4% in 1997 for offences involving ecstasy-type drugs.

46   Most people dealt with for drug offences are male, around 90% in each year. The average age of offenders has remained constant at 25. In 1997 6% were aged under 17, doubling since 1974, and about 25% between 17 and 20 years.

How drug offenders are dealt with

47   The ways that drug offenders are dealt with, and in what numbers and proportions, are set out in Table 2.3. In overall numbers, there has been a four-fold increase between 1985 and 1997. The number of offenders receiving fines has doubled, as has the number sentenced to immediate custody. The number receiving community sentences has increased four-fold in the same period, while the number receiving cautions has increased sixteen-fold.

48   The trend revealed in Figure 2.3 is of a massive increase in the proportion of offenders cautioned. These now account for half of all offenders dealt with. This has been matched by a sustained decrease in the proportion fined. By contrast, the proportion imprisoned or receiving community sentences has remained relatively stable, with some year-on-year variations.

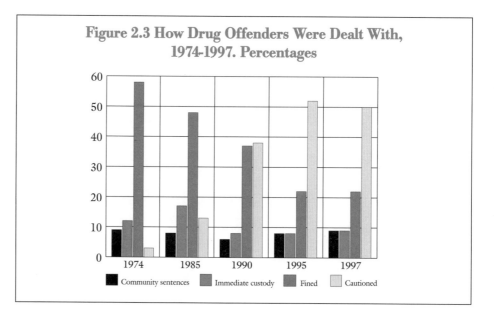

Figure 2.3 How Drug Offenders Were Dealt With, 1974-1997. Percentages

49   The increased use of cautioning clearly dominates the picture. This is largely a result of a preponderance of offenders dealt with for the possession of drugs, especially cannabis. In 1997 for example, 96% of those cautioned for drug offences involved the possession of drugs, and in the same year 58% of those dealt with for cannabis possession were cautioned. Cautions are increasingly used in cases of possession of other drugs: 26% for the possession of cocaine in 1997 as against only 8% in 1990; 23% for heroin in 1997 as against 7 % in 1990; and 33% for amphetamines in 1997 as against 10% in 1990.

Table 2.3 How drug offenders were dealt with[1] in the United Kingdom 1974 to 1997. Numbers and percentages.

	1974		1985		1990		1995		1997	
Cautioned	394	(3%)	3,624	(13%)	17,025	(38%)	48,824	(52%)	56,756	(50%)
Dealt with by compounding	-		362	(1%)	1,184	(3%)	668	(1%)	547	(*)
Fiscal fine	-		-		-		-		484	(*)
Immediate custody[2]	1,531	(12%)	4,535	(17%)	3,402	(8%)	7,086	(8%)	10,422	(9%)
Fined	7,276	(58%)	12,985	(48%)	16,437	(37%)	20,867	(22%)	24,421	(22%)
Community sentence[3]	1,068	(9%)	2,219	(8%)	2,693	(6%)	7,780	(8%)	9,907	(9%)
Absolute/Conditional discharge	1,261	(10%)	1,711	(6%)	2,558	(6%)	6,036	(6%)	7,311	(6%)
Otherwise dealt with	1,001	(8%)	1,522	(6%)	1,623	(4%)	2,370	(3%)	3,308	(3%)
Total[4]	12,532		26,958		44,922		93,631		113,154	

(*) less than 1%

Notes:
1. When a person is found guilty of two or more drug offences at the same court appearance, the sentence or order shown is the most severe penalty.
2. Includes unsuspended imprisonment, partly suspended imprisonment and youth sentences.
3. Includes Combination Orders (since 1993), Community Service Orders, Probation and Supervision Orders.
4. There are small errors in the published totals for 1974 and 1997.

Source: Home Office

50   The use of cautions declines rapidly for the most serious offences. Even so, it remains an option that is sometimes employed over the whole range of offences. In 1997 25% of those dealt with for production offences (which includes the cultivation of cannabis) were cautioned, 10% for supply and 6% for possession with intent to supply unlawfully.

51   Where these more serious drug trafficking offences are concerned, involving importation or supply, offenders are most likely to be brought before the courts and to be subject to more severe penalties, including imprisonment. The percentage of drug offenders in the prison population has increased substantially – from 9% (3,417 out of 34,754) of the sentenced prison population in England and Wales on 30 June 1990, to 15% (7,174 out of 48,674) by the same date in 1997.   The length of prison sentences for importation and supply offences has increased during the 1990s, whereas for other offences it has remained stable.

52   It is important to note, however, that in each year since 1990 over 80% of those found guilty of drug offences were sentenced for possession. Moreover, in terms of the sentencing options available to the courts, the fine remains by far the most commonly used penalty, in spite of its overall decline. In 1997 it still accounted for almost half of all sentences passed by courts for drug offences. In the same year, one-fifth received sentences of immediate imprisonment, the same proportion received community sentences, and the remainder (14%) received conditional or absolute discharges.

53   We should note two other ways of dealing with drug offences: the use (since 1995) of fiscal fines in Scotland and compounding by HM Customs and Excise (see paragraph 41 above). In 1997, the first year for which figures for fiscal fines are available, 499 were accepted, 432 for the possession of cannabis, 60 for the possession of other drugs and 7 for other offences. The percentage of customs cases involving cannabis in which compounding was used increased from 20% in 1985 to 48% in 1990, but has since fallen back to 31% in 1997.

54   In conclusion, the history of sentencing and penalties associated with drug offences is dominated by two features. First the increasing number of offenders, and second a marked trend over the years towards the use of less formal sanctions and penalties. In particular, the caution is used more, diverting offenders away from the courts.

Public attitudes

55   As part of our work, we felt that it was important to try and learn something about public attitudes towards drugs, the harms associated with them, and the role of the law. A survey was commissioned from MORI which provided some surprising responses and proved particularly revealing about attitudes towards drugs in contemporary Britain.

56   The surveys were conducted among adults and school students, and asked a range of questions concerning the perceived harmfulness of different drugs. The adult survey involved face-to-face interviews with 1,645 people aged 16 and 59 years

between 9 – 13 April 1999. The schools survey was conducted between 18
January and 12 February 1999, and collected completed questionnaires from
3,529 pupils aged 11-16 years.

57   One key question was how people assessed the relative harmfulness of different
drugs. Where adults were concerned, substantial majorities of 90 per cent or so
across all age ranges – from 16 to 59 years, judged heroin, cocaine, ecstasy and
amphetamines to be either very or fairly harmful. By contrast, only one-third
judged cannabis to be as harmful, and again this judgement hardly varied with age.
Attitudes tended to vary with age where alcohol and tobacco were concerned, with
a marked tendency to see these substances as increasingly harmful with increasing
age. Among adults from 18 to 59 years, cannabis was seen as by far the least
harmful of all these drugs.

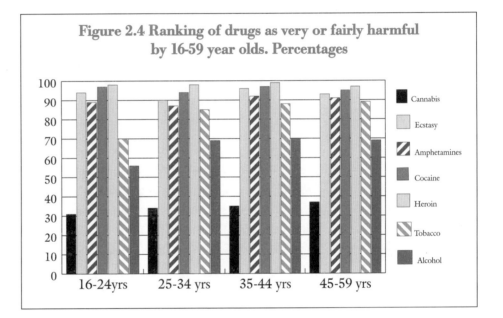

58   Public attitudes, therefore, do not lump all drugs together, but adopt a more
considered view of the harmfulness of different substances; a view, moreover,
which tends to conform with medical and scientific opinion (see Chapter Three,
paragraphs 23 and 24). The one exception to this is that people judge ecstasy to
be almost as harmful as heroin and cocaine, whereas scientific opinion tends to
judge ecstasy as considerably less harmful.

59   In the schools survey, attitudes towards the perceived harmfulness of drugs were
different in important ways. Children aged 11-12 years offered a much simpler
testimony, seeing all illicit drugs (including cannabis) as more or less equally
harmful. In contrast, 11 to 12 year-olds see alcohol and tobacco as relatively much
less harmful, and this view does not change with age among 11-16 year-olds.
Attitudes towards cannabis change considerably as young people grow older – so
that by age 15-16 years they see cannabis in the same way as adults, that is as
among the least harmful of drugs.

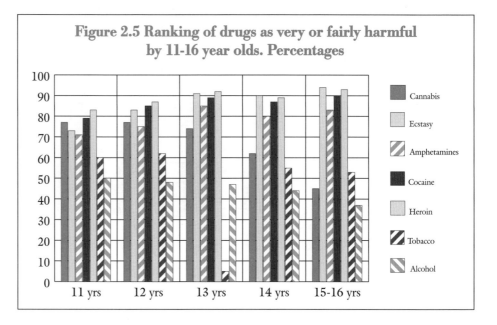

Figure 2.5 Ranking of drugs as very or fairly harmful by 11-16 year olds. Percentages

Legend: Cannabis, Ecstasy, Amphetamines, Cocaine, Heroin, Tobacco, Alcohol

60 Young people also reported increasingly with age that they knew someone of their own age who had smoked cannabis. By age 15-16 years, only about one in ten said that they did not know someone who had used cannabis. Young people of all ages, as with adults, see heroin, cocaine, amphetamines and ecstasy as very harmful.

61 Between the ages of 11 and 16 years the perceptions of children as they grow older gradually move to approximate the views of adults. The exception is attitude to alcohol and tobacco: only adults see these substances as particularly harmful. The most frequent reasons given by both children and adults for people not taking drugs were 'health reason' (33% and 51%) and 'just don't want to take drugs' (27% and 56%). By comparison only 19% of children and 30% of adults mentioned 'illegality' and 12% of children and 17% of adults cited 'fear of being caught by the police'.

62 People did nevertheless want to see strong and effective drug laws. Two-thirds of adults thought that the law against drugs 'is not tough enough', and tended not to agree that the use of drugs was merely a matter of personal choice. Once again, views differed sharply between different drugs. Whereas two-thirds expressed the view that drug laws should be tougher, approximately one-half of all adults felt that the law should be changed so that the use of cannabis was no longer illegal. In the schools survey a higher number of children and young people said that fear of being caught by their parents (21%) was more of an influence than fear of being caught by the police. The latter view was held a little more strongly among younger age groups, although in all age groups a clear majority of those who expressed a view felt that the law with regard to cannabis should be changed.

63 The MORI survey evidence suggests that people view the health consequences of drug use as a more important deterrent than legal controls. They do want strong and effective drug controls, but do not believe that the police alone can be effective in curbing the damage caused by drug misuse. When asked to state what priority the police should give to a variety of different offences, heroin dealing and sexual assaults were seen as by far the most important. They were mentioned by

two-thirds of respondents. Assault, racial violence and drink-driving were mentioned by one-third, with burglary and muggings mentioned by one in five. At the lower end of the spectrum heroin users (as opposed to dealers) were mentioned by only 8%, and cannabis dealers by 9%. Cannabis users, on the other hand, were hardly mentioned at all as a police priority – by less than half of one per cent of respondents.

Table 2.4   **Which three of the following do you think should be the highest priority for the police? Percentages.**

Sexual assaults	71
Dealers who sell heroin	66
Assault	32
Racial violence	32
Drink-driving	32
Burglary	22
Mugging	17
Dealers who sell cannabis	8
Heroin users	8
Vehicle theft	4
Cannabis users	0.5

64   It is clear on this evidence that cannabis stands out as a special case in public attitudes towards drugs in modern Britain. It is seen by adults as by far the least harmful of all drugs, including alcohol and tobacco. The possession of cannabis is seen as the very lowest of priorities for the allocation of police resources. A majority of adults, young and old, even feel that its use should be legalised. Where other drugs are concerned, public opinion fully supports strong drug laws, while emphasising concern with the health risks resulting from drug use. We were particularly impressed by the uniformity of these attitudes towards cannabis and other drugs across different social groups and age groups. Perhaps most surprisingly in terms of the way in which public debate is often constructed, there was no evidence of a 'generation gap' in public attitudes towards the use of cannabis.

65   This last point perhaps indicates as well as anything how far public attitudes towards drug use may have changed in the past thirty years. Unfortunately, there are no directly similar surveys from the past to compare with our own findings. The MORI poll which we commissioned is undoubtedly the most comprehensive survey of its type to be as yet conducted in Britain. Even so, we can offer some idea of how attitudes seem to have changed on some questions, although unfortunately most of these relate only to the legal status of cannabis.

66   Since 1969 surveys of representative samples of the adult population have shown an increasing proportion agreeing with variations on the statement 'Cannabis should be legalised', rising from one in eight in 1969 to one in three in 1997. In the 1990s between 50% and 60% of people who responded to questionnaires in magazines aimed at the young adult market or broadcast by radio stations agreed that cannabis should be 'legalised' or 'decriminalised'. Surveys of chief constables, doctors and Members of Parliament have also found substantial minorities agreeing that the controls on cannabis were too harsh or should be relaxed[16].

67   Our survey therefore falls broadly into line with these others, indicating that while cannabis is seen as one of the least harmful of all drugs, other drugs such as heroin, cocaine, amphetamine or ecstasy are seen differently. Earlier surveys have also shown that the public response to cannabis is markedly different than towards other drugs. A 1995 survey[17], for example, asked 'which drug, if any, that you may not take yourself do you feel its acceptable for others to take if they wish to?' Apart from alcohol and tobacco, cannabis was the most acceptable drug to all age groups, to 40% of 16-19 year-olds, 47% of 20-24 year-olds, 36% of 25-34 year-olds, 25% of 35-54 year-olds. Among 16 to 19 year-olds, the dance drugs, amphetamines (17%), LSD (15%) and ecstasy (12%) were the next most acceptable drugs. In 1998, a similar survey[18] found that among people aged 18-34 years 50% agreed that 'using cannabis is no worse than smoking or drinking' compared with 29% of those aged 35 years and older.

68   In conclusion, earlier surveys have found increasing levels of acceptance of illegal drug use, but restricted almost entirely to the use of cannabis. These surveys invariably find that younger people are more tolerant towards cannabis use. Where our own survey is concerned, although there was undoubtedly less strong support for legal change among older age groups, when asked about the comparative harmfulness of different drugs these age differences all but disappeared.

Conclusions

69   All the indicators point to a steep increase in the number of drug users in the United Kingdom since 1973 when the Misuse of Drugs Act 1971 came into force, although the extent of the increase varies between regions and countries. In particular, there has been a substantial rise in the number of problem drug users, especially of heroin users. Since 1990 the largest increase in problem dug users has occurred amongst those aged under 21. Despite the weaknesses of the data, they are meaningful. They represent the minimum extent of a type of drug use whose harm to the individual and society is definable.

70   The nationally representative self-report surveys indicate there has also been a substantial increase in the number of casual drug users. The use of cannabis dominates the figures, followed by amphetamines. Important additional information from local studies, especially longitudinal studies, shows how the picture of use is changing ahead of national indicators. These surveys indicate that, while cannabis predominates, its use in combination with other drugs (ecstasy, amphetamines, LSD) is not uncommon.

---

[16]R. Newcombe, 'The people on drugs', *Druglink*, (14) Issue 4 (1999), 12-15.
[17]MORI, Modern Britain, survey conducted for the Independent on Sunday newspaper.
[18]ICM survey for The Guardian newspaper.

71   The big divide in drug use is between those under and over 30 years old. Although the onset of use occurs between the ages of 15 and 16, the indicators suggest that the majority of these users are casual drug users who do not go on to become problem drug users. The social profile for the casual drug user is different from that of the problem drug user and shows no significant correlation with deprivation. Early use in combination with deprivation remain the strongest indicators of progression to problem use. However, we do not yet know the implications for adult drug use of the large increase in casual use, especially of stimulants, by young people in the 1990s.

72   It is not surprising that the prevalence of use is mirrored in the statistics on drug seizures and offending against the MDA. Since the first full year of operation of the Misuse of Drugs Act 1971 in 1974 the number of offenders against the MDA and related legislation has risen steadily, more than a ninefold increase. The number of seizures by enforcement agencies and the amounts seized of heroin, cocaine, amphetamines, cannabis and ecstasy have significantly, indeed in some cases dramatically, increased since 1990. Nonetheless the scale of availability as implied by the prevalence of use, especially when set against the reported stability in prices on the street, makes it difficult to avoid the conclusion that efforts to choke off supply have largely failed.

73   The evidence on sentencing indicates that the courts view trafficking offences such as importation, production and supply as serious crimes. However, it seems to be indisputable that enforcement resources are chiefly taken up with possession offences, especially cannabis possession. Even though the decisions by the police, Customs and Excise and the courts to use cautions, compounding and fines reflects more realistically the relatively minor seriousness of these offences, this concentration of effort appears out of line with the attitudes of a significant portion of the public. The findings from our own and previous surveys seem clear: there is majority support for a firm law on drugs alongside substantial and increasing minority support (a third to a half) for relaxation of the law on cannabis. Our own survey indicates that the public's highest priority for enforcement is trafficking in the seriously addictive drugs such as heroin rather than offences reflecting personal use, especially but not exclusively of cannabis.

74   The government's 10-year drug strategy adopted in 1997 urges that resources should be focused on those drugs that do the greatest damage. Indeed, it is the combination of the most dangerous drugs – principally heroin and crack-cocaine – and the forces of social exclusion that provide the greatest challenge to combating drug misuse in Britain in the new millennium. In a recent report the Advisory Council on the Misuse of Drugs observed that:

> 'We thus assert without any of the familiar hedging with "on the one hand but on the other", that on strong balance of probability deprivation is today in Britain likely often to make a significant causal contribution to the cause, complication and intractability of damaging kinds of drug misuse... We want now and in the future to see deprivation given its full and proper place in all considerations of drug prevention policy, held in that policy consciousness, and not let slip from sight' [19]

---

[19] *Drug Misuse and the Environment, London, The Stationery Office 1998.*
Paragraphs 9.49 and 9.59.

We believe this to be an important conclusion, and stress that tackling problem drug use must always also involve tackling social deprivation.

75   The flaws and gaps in the information and research base necessary to investigate adequately the extent of drug use and its control are striking. Since doctors are no longer required to notify their addict patients the national data on the scale and changes in problem drug use over time are arguably less adequate than they were. Procedures for mapping local variations in drug use are seriously wanting. Available information provides little insight into how drug use behaviours are formed or changed, or on the pathways from casual to problem use. A commitment to longitudinal studies is needed.

76   Equally striking is the relative absence of detailed cost information about drug use. From our investigations estimates of drug related healthcare, enforcement and other social service costs appear rudimentary. Such information, together with the results of systematic evaluations of prevention, treatment and control initiatives, would facilitate a realistic assessment of drug control and prevention strategies. None of the attitude surveys throw any light on the influence, if any, of the law in controlling illicit drug use. The impact of the law may appear disappointingly limited but the majority of the population does not appear to take drugs and it may be that the law has some effect on some of them

77   As a matter of priority, we recommend that renewed attention is given to the information and research base which facilitates understanding of the evolving picture of drug use and the cost effectiveness of welfare and control responses. Routine statistics should be improved to reduce gaps in the understanding of the scale, nature and extent of drug use. Enforcement and treatment policies should be evaluated thoroughly, making full use of the available range of social science research methods.

Chapter Three: Classes and Schedules

Introduction

1   The division of controlled drugs into three Classes is a central feature of the Misuse of Drugs Act 1971 (MDA). The Classes are linked to maximum penalties in a descending order of severity, from A to C. The three-tier classification was designed to make it possible to control particular drugs according to their comparative harmfulness either to individuals or to society at large when they were misused. This was a new departure. In introducing the legislation in 1970, the Home Secretary, Mr. Callaghan, said[1]

> 'The object here is to make, so far as possible, a more sensible differentiation between drugs. It will divide them according to their accepted dangers and harmfulness in the light of current knowledge and it will provide for changes to be made in the classification in the light of new scientific knowledge.'

We have given considerable attention to this area because of the importance of getting it right if the law is to be credible, proportionate and just and if it is to be able to support accurate education in the harmfulness of drugs.

The main drugs in Classes A, B and C

Class A
Includes cannabinol and cannabinol derivatives[1], cocaine (including 'crack'), dipipanone, ecstasy and related compounds[2], heroin, LSD, magic mushrooms, methadone, morphine, opium, pethidine and phenylcyclidine.

Class B drugs which are prepared for injection are classed as Class A.

Class B
Includes amphetamines, barbiturates, cannabis (herbal), cannabis (resin), codeine, dihydrocodeine and methylamphetamine

Class C
Includes anabolic steroids, benzodiazepines, buprenorphine, diethylpropion, mazindol, pemoline and phentermine.

Notes: 1   These include a variety of natural and synthetic cannabinoids, a family of substances based on the same core chemical structure. The most active and potent of these is d9-tetrahydrocannabinol (d9THC), which is the main psychoactive ingredient of all forms of cannabis, although a number of other cannabinoids are also psychoactive.
         2   Ecstasy is a synthetic amphetamine derivative, methylenedioxymethylamphetamine (MDMA). It is often confused with related compounds such as ethylenedioxymetamphetamine (EVE) and dioxymethylamphetamine (DMA).

Penalties

2   The Classes are related to the maximum penalties set out for each MDA offence in Schedule 4. They are therefore central to the MDA's aim of differentiating offences according to the particular drug involved. Maximum penalties are not the standard or average penalty to which offenders are liable in all cases: rather they

---

[1] *Hansard*, House of Commons, 25th March 1970.

allow the courts discretion when dealing with individual cases. Very few offences should or do attract the maximum penalty. Nevertheless these penalties must have an influence on the courts. Moreover in the case of trafficking offences involving Class A drugs, there is under the Crime Sentences Act 1997, a mandatory minimum sentence of seven years custody for the third such offence. Putting a drug in a higher Class must therefore tend to result in higher sentences for offences related to it. It is important that a drug's place in its Class is fully justified. We have sought to establish criteria for classification that are as far as possible objective and clear.

Developments since 1971

3   When the United Nations Convention on Psychotropic Drugs was adopted in 1971, the main drugs brought under international control were already listed in the MDA. They had been controlled under United Kingdom legislation since the passage of the Drugs (Prevention of Misuse) Act 1964. Nevertheless numerous additions have been made to the Classes over the years by order. Among these are the inclusion of ecstasy in Class A in 1977, barbiturates in Class B in 1984, certain tranquillisers, particularly the benzodiazepines (temazepam is probably the most often used illicitly) in Class C in 1985 and anabolic steroids in Class C in 1996.

4   Transfers between Classes on the other hand have occurred only twice. The first occasion was the transfer of nicodicodine from Class A to Class B in 1973. The second followed the only full review of the Classes carried out since 1971 by the Advisory Council on the Misuse of Drugs[2]. The Council was broadly satisfied with the classification of controlled drugs. It made only two recommendations: that cannabis and cannabis resin be transferred from Class B to Class C, which was not implemented, and that methaqualone (a sedative) be moved from Class C to Class B, which was.

Criteria for classifying drugs

5   The explicit criteria in section 1 (2) of the MDA are (1) whether the drug is being misused or (2) whether it is likely to be misused and (3) whether the misuse in either case is having or could have harmful effects sufficient to constitute a social problem. There appears to be no explicit criterion for deciding which drugs are more harmful than others and so should go in Class A rather than B or C. The Council, however, deduced that the nature of the mischief to which misuse might give rise was a criterion implicit in the threefold classification and its link to penalties. As it said,

> 'The classification of drugs under Schedule 2 exists solely to determine which scale of penalties shall be applicable to the various offences involving individual drugs. Schedules 2 and 4 together serve as an indication to the police and the courts of the importance which Parliament attaches to dealing with the mischief caused by the misuse of a particular drug'[3].

---

[2] *Report on a Review of the Classification of Controlled Drugs and of Penalties under Schedules 2 and 4 of the Misuse of Drugs Act 1971*, London, Home Office 1979.
[3] See paragraph 3.7 of the report cited in the preceding note.

Other European countries

6 Although not required by the international conventions, most other European countries divide illicit drugs into Classes but none use the precise division found in the MDA and only three (Italy, the Netherlands and Portugal) relate the Classes to maximum penalties. It seems that it is usually left to the courts to reflect the relative harm of the drug in the sentences passed. In such cases the main purpose served by the classification seems more akin to that of the Schedules to the Misuse of Drugs Regulations 1985, which we discuss below.

Classification systems in other European countries

Austria, Belgium, Luxembourg   No formal legal classes.

Denmark Five Classes.
A	cannabis, heroin, prepared opium
B	cocaine, ecstasy, amphetamines, methadone
C	codeine
D	barbiturates
E	tranquillisers

Finland Ten Classes.

Narcotics
I	heroin, cannabis, methadone, morphine, etc.
II	propiram, codeine, etc.
III	preparations containing drugs.
IV	drugs in Class I with no medical uses

Psychotropic substances
I	MDA, LSD, MDMA, etc.
II	amphetamines, THC, etc.
III	barbiturates
IV	benzodiazepines etc.

Precursors
I	ephedrine, lysergic acid
II	acetone, piperidine.

France Four Classes.
I	hallucinogens
II	amphetamines
III	barbiturates and buprenorphine
IV	benzodiazepines and phenobarbitol

Germany Three Classes.
I	Not for medical or industrial use: heroin, cannabis, LSD
II	For industrial use but not available on prescription: coca leaves
III	For industrial and medical use on special prescription: morphine, methadone.

Greece Four Classes.
I	cannabis, heroin, LSD and other hallucinogens
II	cocaine, methadone, opium
III	amphetamines
IV	barbiturates, tranquillisers

Classification systems in other European countries continued

Ireland Five Classes.
- I   cannabis, LSD, mescaline, opium
- II   cocaine, heroin, methadone, morphine
- III & IV other psychotropic substances
- V   specific preparations of drugs

Italy Six Classes.
- I   opium, cocaine, hallucinogens, some amphetamines
- II   cannabis
- III   barbiturates
- IV   medicinal substances
- V   preparations of substances mentioned at I to III
- VI   antidepressants, stimulants

The Netherlands Two main Classes.
- I   <u>Drugs which pose unacceptable risks</u> opiates, coca derivatives, cannabis oil, codeine, ecstasy, amphetamine, LSD, etc.
- II   <u>Other drugs</u> cannabis, barbiturates, tranquillisers

Portugal Six main Classes.
- I   opiates, coca and derivatives, cannabis and derivatives
- II   hallucinogens, amphetamines, barbiturates
- III   specific preparations
- IV   tranquillisers and analgesics
- V & VI precursors

Spain   Drugs placed under control as in UN Conventions

Sweden Five Classes.
- I   narcotics with no medical uses
- II   narcotics with medical uses
- III   codeine
- IV   barbiturates, benzodiazepines
- V   narcotics as defined by Swedish law but not restricted by international conventions

Source: Annual Report on the State of the Drugs Problem in the European Union 1997, European Monitoring Centre for Drugs and Drug Addiction, Luxembourg 1997.

Our recommended approach

7   We believe that the present classification of drugs in the MDA should be reviewed to take account of modern developments in medical, scientific and sociological knowledge. The main criterion should continue to be that of dangerousness but the criteria should be made clear. The relative dangerousness of drugs is determined by a number of factors, some applying to the individual, others to society. The main justification for controlling drugs lies in the harm that their use causes to society. However, we should make it clear that, as a matter of principle, it is right for the law to take into account harm that drugs cause to users themselves,

as well as to other people affected by users or to the community at large. It is widely agreed that there are cases in which the law may properly try to protect people from harming themselves. These are cases – seatbelts and motorcyclists' helmets are examples – in which the damage is serious, almost always comes about unintentionally, and is hard to reverse. This is the kind of risk that is associated in varying degrees with dangerous drugs, and the case is even stronger to the extent that they take away the power of choice. For these reasons, we think, as most people do, that the law should take into account the harms that drugs do to the people who use them. In any case, it is impossible in fact to separate harms to users from harms to others; self-inflicted damage usually results in costs to others. The harm to the individual as a consequence of the pharmacological effects of a drug lends itself best to objective evaluation. Initially at least, this harm is likely to be the best indicator of how strictly a drug needs to be controlled.

8   Personal harm may be assessed on the basis of four factors:

   i)   risks of the drug itself: acute (short-term) and chronic (long-term) toxicity;

   ii)   risks due to the route of use;

   iii) extent to which the drug controls behaviour (addictiveness/dependency);

   iv)   ease of stopping.

The relative dangers of each factor vary from drug to drug. For example, heroin is highly toxic acutely but may cause little chronic toxicity provided it is used in a sterile fashion. The benzodiazepines have relatively little acute toxicity but may be difficult to stop taking after long-term use.

Acute toxicity

9   The acute toxicity of a drug determines the risk of death or severe and immediate symptoms following an overdose. Data on the lethal dose that kills 50% of individuals exposed to it (LD50) is available for all illicit drugs expressed as units of the drug per kilogram of body weight on the basis of experiments on animals. It is obviously more difficult to estimate the absolute value of the LD50 dose for humans. In terms of units of drug per kilogram of body weight it is probably much lower in humans than in animals, although the same rank order of lethality probably applies as with animals. On the basis of such data it is clear that the risk of overdose is highest for heroin, other opiates and cocaine – all more dangerous than alcohol in this respect. It is lowest for cannabis. Amphetamines, ecstasy, psychedelic drugs and benzodiazepines come somewhere in between.

10   It is also possible to evaluate the safety of drugs indirectly through estimates of mortality rates in the population of users. Although the results are subject to considerable measurement errors, particularly in estimating the number of users, they can give an idea of the relative risks of dying after drug use. We discuss the implications for ecstasy in particular in paragraphs 29 and 30 below.

Chronic health risks

11   This is harder to gauge, especially with drugs that have only recently become popular. More objective measures include mortality and morbidity statistics; less objective ones are clinical expert opinions. The safety approach used by drug regulatory authorities before licensing drugs for clinical use relies on the detection of pathological changes found after chronic administration in animals. Such studies have been done for many of the drugs controlled by the MDA, though not to our knowledge for cocaine, LSD or other psychedelics. On the basis of present knowledge, cannabis may lead in the long term to respiratory diseases in the same way as tobacco. Benzodiazepines present the lowest risks of long-term health damage and the stimulant drugs the highest. The emerging evidence about ecstasy is that it may cause more long-term damage than once supposed. The long-term risks of alcohol and tobacco, however, are also as high as from some illicit drugs. The psychedelic drugs (other than ecstasy) on present (limited) evidence carry fewer chronic health risks. This is an area that needs to be kept under continuing review in order to take account of advances in medical and scientific knowledge as they are made.

Route of use

12   The route of use predicts the nature and severity of the physical damage that a drug can cause as well as its addictiveness. Intravenous use (injecting) dramatically increases the risk of infections when sterile needles and syringes are not available. Many regular intravenous drug users are hepatitis C positive and up to 20% of them will develop progressive destructive cirrhosis of the liver. A variable proportion are HIV positive and will be at high risk of developing AIDS. The exceptional speed of access that injecting gives to many body organs also results in increased risks of acute toxicity and overdose.

13   Drugs which are readily injected are therefore more dangerous than others. They fall into four groups. The first of these comprises opiates, the second stimulants in liquid forms, including ampoules. Third are highly soluble drugs like buprenorphine that can easily be made into solutions from tablets. Finally there are less soluble drugs that are dissolved in solvents (as temazepam in gel capsule form) or temazepam and other benzodiazepines crushed and mixed with water.

14   Other ways of taking drugs have their own risks if taken over a prolonged period. Smoking can lead to lung and heart disease, snorting and chewing to nose and mouth cancer. Even drugs that are swallowed (usually the safest method) may cause stomach cancer.

Dependence and addiction

15   These terms overlap and are difficult to define. Both include a wide range of experiences and phenomena associated with problem drug use. Among them is the process of adaptation to drug use, known as tolerance, which results in the need to take ever larger doses of the drug to achieve the same effect. There may also be unpleasant and sometimes dangerous physical symptoms once the drug is stopped.

These withdrawal symptoms are alleviated by taking the drug again. This relief use is a major reason for the continued use of certain drugs. The cycle of dependence becomes stronger the longer the use of the drug goes on.

16   These forms of dependence are known as physical dependence and are associated with all the drugs controlled by the MDA with the possible exception of LSD, other psychedelics and ecstasy. Physical dependence may arise without tolerance and without increasing the dosage. This has been called normal dose dependence and is found particularly in the benzodiazepines. It is, however, hard to measure the severity of the withdrawal symptoms in such cases since they are often confused with the re-emergence of the symptoms of the disorders for which the drug was prescribed.

17   Perhaps what most people understand by addiction is the need to keep on taking the drug for its pleasurable effects. The pleasure that a drug produces leads to the desire to use it again; the effect is called reinforcement. The degree of pleasure relates to the action of the drug on the brain's chemical systems and varies with the chemical structure of drugs even within the same family. This is why heroin gives more pleasure than other opiates such as codeine or buprenorphine. The process by which drug dependence is achieved in this way is termed psychological dependence and in its extreme form is called craving.

18   Physical and psychological dependence are both likely to be present to some extent in the careers of drug users. Research evidence suggests that early in a drug user's career pleasure-seeking is the main motivation for continued use whereas later on the wish to avoid withdrawal symptoms predominates. The propensity of a drug to cause craving and the difficulty that users find in stopping are both therefore important indicators of risk. So is the ease with which the symptoms concerned are re-established if the drug is taken again after a period of abstinence.

Social risks

19   Some forms of social harm are a direct consequence of intoxication, for example road traffic accidents. Others come from addiction and dependence: the drug controls behaviour to an extent that has detrimental effects on all aspects of social functioning. In severe cases this can lead to complete personal collapse with loss of job, family and ability to look after oneself. It may also lead to acquisitive crime in order to obtain the funds to buy further supplies of the drug. A third area relates to the medical complications and the costs of treating drug use and dependence.

20   Social harm is hard to quantify. The health care impact is difficult to estimate because the costs of treating addiction are fixed arbitrarily by the availability of treatment resources. Also they are only a fraction of the full medical costs. Unknown extra costs include those due to accidents, infections and mental illness. Other social costs, for example from crime, are hard to measure because it may not always be the drug use that leads to the commission of criminal offences[4]. It is, however, possible to reach a reasoned assessment of relative social harm without precisely quantified estimates. The addictive and dependency potential of a drug can be used to a large extent as a proxy for the social risks - a highly addictive drug will lead to a great deal of social harm.

---

[4]The evidence for the association between drugs and crime is assembled in *Drug-driven Crime: A factual and statistical analysis.* London, NACRO 1999, and discussed further in this report in Chapters Two (paragraphs 5 and 6), Seven (paragraph 19) and Eight (paragraphs 2 to 9 and 14).

21 Such evidence as there is suggests that the health and other social costs attributable to illicit drugs are small compared with the health and social costs of alcohol and tobacco. A recent French study[5] has estimated that 6% of the costs of responding to social problems caused by drugs are attributable to illicit drugs as compared with 40% to tobacco and 54% to alcohol.

Our assessment of the relative harms of drugs

22 We have sought to rank controlled drugs on the basis of the available pharmacological and other evidence of each drug's likelihood of causing the following physical and social problems:

i) acute (i.e. immediate) physical harm, including the risk of overdose;

ii) physical harm from chronic (i.e. longer-term) use;

iii) ease with which drug may be injected;

iv) likelihood of drug leading to dependence and addiction;

v) physical withdrawal symptoms;

vi) psychological withdrawal symptoms;

vii) risk of social harm through intoxication;

viii) risk of causing other social problems;

ix) risk of medical costs arising.

23 We consulted the members of the Royal College of Psychiatrists' Faculty of Substance Misuse about the relative harmfulness of controlled drugs. We received replies from 29 out of 77 of them. Although we did not ask them specifically how they would classify the drugs concerned, their replies showed a high degree of consensus over the ranking of drugs by harmfulness. No-one disputes the position of heroin and cocaine at the top of the list. Methadone, amphetamines, barbiturates and temazepam when used intravenously are, in the consensus view of those whom we consulted, in the top seven (as is alcohol). Ecstasy, LSD, steroids and cannabis come in the last five (below tobacco). Buprenorphine, codeine and benzodiazepines other than temazepam are in-between.

24 Assessing our results in the light of these responses seems to us to point to the following implications for the present Classes. To put things in perspective, we show in square brackets where alcohol and tobacco might come in the Classes if they were drugs controlled under the MDA.

Main drugs and their Classes

Class A
cocaine
heroin
methadone
other opiates in pure form
amphetamines in injectable form
[alcohol]

---

[5]P. Kopp, *Le Cout Social des Drogues Licites (Alcool et Tabac) et Illicites*, Paris, OFDT and MILDT 1999.

Class B

amphetamines other than injectable

barbiturates

buprenorphine

codeine

ecstasy and ecstasy-type drugs

LSD

[tobacco]

Class C

cannabinol and cannabinol derivatives

benzodiazepines

cannabis

Our conclusions on classification

Number of Classes

25 We have considered whether three Classes of drug are still appropriate. One advantage of doing away with Classes altogether would be that attention would focus on the offences themselves irrespective of the drug concerned. Reducing the number of Classes to two on the other hand would enable a clear division to be opened up between the seriously dangerous and the less harmful drugs. This is the approach of the Netherlands, where heroin, cocaine, amphetamines, ecstasy and other drugs described as posing unacceptable risks are on one list while a second list contains cannabis, most barbiturates and most tranquillisers.

26 We are not inclined to abolish the Classes altogether. We consider that the differences between drugs are important, and need to be credibly reflected in our law if penalties are to be proportionate to a drug's harm. We are impressed with the Netherlands' determination to draw a clear and meaningful distinction between dangerous and less harmful drugs; but we doubt whether it accurately reflects the complexity of the situation. The Netherlands claims, with considerable justification, to have created clear blue water between cannabis and heroin. We doubt whether they can make the same claim in respect of other drugs, especially ecstasy, which are widely used in the Netherlands. These seem to us to be in a position intermediate between the highly dangerous and addictive drugs like heroin and the less harmful ones like cannabis. The model of three Classes offered by the MDA enables this to be reflected and we therefore believe that it should be retained.

27 In recommending the retention of three Classes, we also recommend the transfer of certain drugs between Classes in accordance with the analysis in paragraphs 7 to 24 above. We further propose clear criteria for the future to govern additions to and transfers between the Classes.

Transfers of drugs between Classes

28 The analysis above demonstrates in our view the extent to which the MDA's Classes fail to reflect the most up-to-date medical and scientific knowledge. Drugs

which seem clearly to be in too high a Class include ecstasy (as suggested to us by the Association of Chief Police Officers (ACPO)), LSD, cannabinol and its derivatives such as d-9 THC, and cannabis. The risks associated with buprenorphine, on the other hand, seem to us to make it appropriate to Class B rather than Class C.

29   We recognise that there will be concern over the prospect of ecstasy being moved to Class B. We understand this. Overall, however, the best estimates of the toxicity of ecstasy and related compounds suggest that they are considerably less dangerous in both acute and chronic use than Class A drugs of the opiate or cocaine type. Although deaths from ecstasy are highly publicised, it probably kills fewer than 10 people each year which, though deeply distressing for the surviving relatives and friends, is a small percentage of the many thousands of people who use it each week. Nor is it always clear whether the deaths are caused by ecstasy itself, another substance taken by mistake for it or in combination with it, or the circumstances surrounding its use – overexertion followed by hyperthermia, dehydration or excessive rehydration. Although ecstasy in high doses can cause such effects directly, in many cases they are due to environmental aspects of the dance club scene, particularly overcrowding, overheating, poor availability of cool-out rooms, and restrictions on or the high cost of drinks.

30   Population safety comparisons suggest that ecstasy may be several thousand times less dangerous than heroin, although the exact figure cannot be established with certainty. There is little evidence of craving or withdrawal compared with opiates and cocaine. Ecstasy and its related compounds do not therefore seem to be as addictive in the same sense as these other more dangerous Class A drugs. These observations coupled with other evidence across the range of factors set out in paragraph 22 persuade us that ecstasy and related compounds are significantly less harmful than the other Class A drugs. We therefore recommend that they be transferred to Class B. We are particularly concerned that having them in the same Class as heroin and cocaine gives a message paradoxically opposite to that intended: regular ecstasy users, knowing that it causes them few ill effects, may make similar assumptions about the other Class A drugs.

31   We have also considered in detail the position in the Classes of cannabinols and their derivatives as distinct from the cannabis plant in its natural state. A variety of substances appears to be covered: there are over 60 cannabinoids identified as unique to the cannabis plant and, in addition, several synthetic cannabinoids are available. There is, however, no evidence of widespread illicit use nor of significant harm stemming from use. The British Medical Association state

> 'The acute toxicity of cannabinoids is extremely low: they are very safe drugs and no deaths have been directly attributed to their recreational or therapeutic use' [6]

There is therefore little justification for their place in Class A and the question for us is whether they should be placed in Class B or, with the plant forms of cannabis, in Class C. The most potent of the substances concerned is d9-tetrahydrocannabinol (THC) and we have considered whether to distinguish

---

[6] *Therapeutic use of cannabis,* Amsterdam, Harwood Academic Publishers 1997, page 65.

between cannabinols on the basis of the concentration of THC in them. No other drug, however, is differentiated on the basis of potency and it would often be impracticable for offenders and law enforcers alike to distinguish among the different forms on such a basis. Since the risk of cannabinol and its derivatives seems on present evidence to be comparable with the plant forms of cannabis, we recommend that they should be in the same Class as herbal cannabis and cannabis resin – Class C.

32   The position of benzodiazepines is also problematic. Their intravenous use is one of the more worrying developments in illicit drug use over the past decade or more. Liquid filled or wax capsules are not now easily available in the United Kingdom. But the habit of injecting benzodiazepines remains relatively common, with crushed tablets of temazepam and diazepam in water being the most popular. Efforts should be made to limit the intravenous use of these drugs. Progress has already been made in this direction by the transfer of temazepam to Schedule 3 of the Regulations (see paragraph 44). We wish to await evidence of the effect of this change before recommending further amendments to the classification or scheduling of benzodiazepines. In the meantime, we recommend that the Government encourage the development and manufacture of benzodiazepines in combination with an antagonist, such as flumazenil. This would block the 'high' when used intravenously but would not affect the therapeutic response when taken orally. We further recommend that doctors are encouraged to prescribe the less abused benzodiazepines and non-benzodiazepine alternatives.

33   We also draw attention to the need for a more appropriate classification of buprenorphine. This is a synthetic opiate painkiller that is less addictive and less likely to lead to overdose than strong opiates such as heroin and morphine. The drug was originally used in low dose tablets for severe pain but higher dose tablets are now available as an alternative to methadone. Buprenorphine tablets can be dissolved in water and injected. For this reason, and because high strength tablets are likely to become more common, we recommend moving buprenorphine from Class C to Class B. However, when buprenorphine is prepared in combination with an antagonist, naloxone, the risk of intravenous use is markedly reduced. We would encourage the use of this combination in preference to the pure tablets and recommend that it remain in Class C when in this form.

34   Given the ranking that alcohol and tobacco have in the order of dangerous drugs, it is an obvious question why they and drugs controlled under the MDA should not be treated similarly: either alcohol and tobacco should be added to the appropriate Classes under the MDA or drugs that are no more dangerous than they should be treated as alcohol and tobacco are now treated. We resist this argument. In the first place, it is simply a fact that the use of alcohol and tobacco is so widespread and familiar that an attempt to prohibit their supply by law would lead to widespread resentment and law-breaking (as happened with the Prohibition experiment in the United States from 1920-33). Conversely, the present law against the drugs controlled by the MDA enjoys widespread public acceptance, with the exception of certain aspects of its operation against cannabis.

35   The cases of alcohol and tobacco are in any case not the same. Smoking tobacco is widely regarded as a bad and dangerous habit. Many who smoke wish that they could stop and measures are taken to prevent smoking in public places, to limit advertising and so on. It is a reasonable social aim that the use of tobacco should eventually disappear, even though that aim cannot appropriately be pursued by legal prohibition. Alcohol is a more complicated case. Although it is a dangerous drug and causes enormous social costs and harm, it is also used by many people moderately and non-destructively. It is strictly the misuse of alcohol that needs to be prevented, and while the ways in which this can best be done may be debated, control under the MDA is not one of them.

36   In summary, therefore, we recommend:

i)   the transfer of ecstasy and related compounds from Class A to Class B;

ii)   the transfer of LSD from Class A to Class B;

iii) the transfer of cannabinols such as d-9 THC from Class A to Class C;

iv)   the transfer of buprenorphine from Class C to Class B[7];

v)   the transfer of herbal cannabis and cannabis resin from Class B to Class C.

Future criteria

37   The MDA itself indicates certain criteria for classifying drugs in section 1 (2), namely whether a particular drug is subject or likely to be subject to misuse sufficient to cause a social problem. Since misuse is in effect defined as the taking of a drug by an individual, both individual and social harm are involved. The existence of three Classes linked to penalties suggests that the nature and seriousness of the individual and social harm concerned are important criteria for determining whether a particular drug is placed in Class A, B or C. But the Act is not specific on how individual or social harm should be measured or on how the cut-off points between Classes should be determined. The Advisory Council were unable to be more specific in their 1979 report[8], nor did they explain on what basis they concluded that the then Classes were broadly acceptable.

38   The assessment of some features must remain subjective but we believe that it is possible to reach an objective estimate of relative harmfulness by assessing drugs against the following factors (discussed in detail above):

i)   their potential for leading to dependency and addiction;

ii)   toxicity;

iii) risk of overdose;

iv)   risk to life and health in longer term;

v)   injectability;

vi)   association with crime;

vii) association with problems for communities;

viii) public health costs.

---

[7] We understand that buprenorphine may become available in combination with naloxone, making it safer to use. We would be content to see that combination included in Class C.
[8] See paragraph 4.

39   Class A drugs will normally demonstrate most (not necessarily all) the above factors to a high degree. The benchmark drugs are heroin and cocaine and if comparison with other drugs suggests that they pose equivalent risks then there should be no hesitation in putting them in Class A. Class A should be seen as containing the most dangerous and harmful drugs.

40   Class B drugs will also display one or more of the factors listed above but not as many nor to the same degree. The benchmark drugs are the amphetamines and the barbiturates. These drugs are all harmful but not to the extent of the drugs to be found in Class A. To put the risks in context, if alcohol and tobacco were assessed for control under the MDA using these criteria, alcohol would be classed as B bordering on A, while cigarettes would probably be on the borderline between B and C.

41   The drugs in Class C will score relatively low on the factors listed and demonstrate fewer of them. That is not to say that they are harmless, but on any reasonable scale of risk they must rank lower than other drugs. While controls are justified, offences involving them should not attract penalties as high as the drugs in Classes A and B.

Relationship of Classes to Schedules in the Misuse of Drugs Regulations 1985

42   The Classes in Schedule 2 to the MDA are often confused with the Schedules to the Regulations made under section 7. There are indeed interactions but the main purpose of the Schedules is quite different. They are part of Regulations whose intention is to ensure that the appropriate exemptions are made from the offence provisions of the Act. The Regulations therefore:

(i)   identify those who may handle particular drugs (e.g. doctors, pharmacists, police officers, patients, and in some cases anyone);

(ii) describe the circumstances in which drugs may be handled (e.g. possession on prescription, general authority to supply);

(iii) control the purposes for which a particular drug may be applied (e.g. retail pharmacy, laboratory use, treatment);

(iv) regulate where a drug may be produced or supplied (e.g. a laboratory or a nursing home).

In these ways the Regulations ensure that legitimate activities are exempted from the relevant offence provisions of the MDA. What the Act prohibits, the Regulations allow.

43   The Schedules to the 1985 Regulations work as follows:

Schedule 1 lists drugs that may only be used under licence for medical or scientific research. The drugs in this Schedule include ecstasy, LSD, raw opium, psilocin, cannabis and cannabis resin.

These drugs, which come from both Class A and Class B, are also designated separately by order under section 7 (4) as drugs whose production, supply and possession is unlawful except for purposes of research or other special purposes.

The drugs in this Schedule, irrespective of whether they are in Class A or Class B, are not available on prescription. Except under licence their importation, exportation, production, possession and supply are offences.

Schedule 2 specifies the drugs to which a number of controls over prescription, secure storage, and record keeping apply. It is the longest Schedule in the Regulations. The drugs contained in it are a mixture of Class A and Class B drugs but the requirements are the same regardless of Class.

The drugs in this Schedule include amphetamine, cocaine, heroin, methadone, morphine, pethidine and quinalbarbitone.

The drugs in this Schedule may be prescribed and lawfully supplied and possessed when on prescription. Otherwise supply and possession, together with importation, exportation and production, are offences except under licence.

Schedule 3 lists drugs to which a less elaborate range of controls applies. More paperwork and tighter security precautions are needed for Schedule 2 drugs than for those in Schedule 3. The drugs contained in this Schedule include most barbiturates, buprenorphine, diethylpropion, mazindol, phentermine and temazepam.

These drugs can only be possessed lawfully by a person with a prescription. Uniquely, the prescription requirements for temazepam are less stringent than for the other drugs in the Schedule. Because it is exempted from Regulation 15, the same prescribing requirements apply to it as when it was a drug in Schedule 4.

Schedule 4 lists drugs which may be lawfully possessed by anyone provided they are in the form of medicinal products. They are subject to far fewer administrative controls or criminal sanctions.

The Schedule is in two parts. Part I includes anabolic steroids. Part II includes the benzodiazepines (except temazepam) and pemoline.

Schedule 4 drugs may be lawfully possessed by anyone, even without a prescription, provided they are in the form of medicinal products. The drugs in Part I may also be lawfully imported or exported if they are in the form of such products for self-administration. The drugs in Part II may be freely imported or exported whether they are in the form of medicinal products or not.

Schedule 5 contains very weak preparations or products which may be freely imported, exported or possessed. Authority is, however, needed for their production or supply.

44 Moving a drug from one Schedule to another may have the effect of making possession of that drug a criminal offence when previously it was not, or vice versa. Thus for example the unauthorised possession of temazepam is now a criminal offence under section 5 of the Act by virtue of its transfer from Schedule 4 to Schedule 3 of the Regulations. At the same time it was exempted from Regulation 15, which meant that the relatively tight prescription requirements of the MDA were inapplicable. Temazepam was and remains obtainable only on prescription

but the rules that apply are those of the Medicines Act 1968 not the MDA. Had the MDA requirements applied, an unacceptable extra burden would have been placed on doctors, who prescribe substantial amounts of temazepam. When flunitrazepam was similarly transferred from Schedule 4 to Schedule 3 in 1998, there was no similar exemption made from Regulation

45   It is also possible to transfer by regulation a drug from a more to a less restrictive Schedule. This was done with dronabinol (synthetic THC in sesame oil), which can alleviate some of the adverse effects of chemotherapy. It used to be treated as a cannabinol derivative, a Class A drug that appeared in Schedule 1 of the Misuse of Drugs Regulations 1985. It therefore could not be prescribed by doctors - its only possible legitimate use was in research licensed by the Secretary of State. Following the advice of the World Health Organisation, the United Nations Commission on Narcotic Drugs amended the 1971 convention in such a way that the United Kingdom Government was able to move dronabinol to Schedule 2 of the Regulations. This means that doctors can prescribe dronabinol on a tightly controlled basis. If other cannabinols are to be made available for therapeutic use, a similar process will need to be followed. Herbal cannabis and cannabis resin, however, could be moved from Schedule 1 to Schedule 2 without prior action by the World Health Organisation and United Nations because they are less rigorously controlled under the 1961 convention[9].

Early warning and monitoring

46   We envisage that the Advisory Council for the Misuse of Drugs will continue to be the body that has the statutory responsibility for considering and making recommendations to Ministers on the classification of new drugs and for keeping the existing Classes under review. It is not clear how much attention it has given to the latter since 1979. Nor is it clear from its 1979 report[10] whether it considered the factors we have discussed above and if so what weight it gave them. We recommend that future reports from the Council should clearly state its methods and findings on such matters.

47   We have seen no evidence of effective early warning arrangements in the United Kingdom. Nor do they appear to feature in the national strategy. There seems to have even been a step backwards: information from the Department of Health's regional data bases reaches the centre with greater delay than used to be the case with notifications to the Chief Medical Officer at the Home Office. A reliable and fast-working system is badly needed to identify new drugs that may be causing problems and need to be brought under control, perhaps through special arrangements for emergency scheduling. The latter need arises particularly from the speed and ease with which new synthetic or 'designer' drugs can be manufactured and marketed. Good early warning systems are also required to keep track of changing trends in the use of existing drugs[11], particularly the emergence or re-emergence of prescription drugs on a scale that may lead to serious health and social problems and so possibly to a need to reconsider their classification under the MDA.

---

[9]See Chapter Seven, paragraphs 62 to 64.
[10]See paragraph 4.
[11]See H. Parker, C. Bury, R. Egginton *New Heroin Outbreaks Amongst Young People in England & Wales*, Police Research Group Crime Detection and Prevention Series Paper 92, London, Home Office 1998, pages 9-11

48   Effective early warning arrangements exist in the Netherlands (where the arrangements for pill testing help early identification of substances that may pose risks) and in the United States. The main systems of drug warning and monitoring in the United States are:

i)   The Drug Abuse Warning Network (DAWN), sponsored by the Department of Health and Human Services. Using reports from representative hospital emergency departments and coroner's offices, it monitors trends in drug-related episodes and deaths, the health consequences of drug use, and changes in its nature and extent.

ii)   Arrestee Drug Abuse Monitoring (ADAM), funded by the United States National Institute of Justice. This provides information on the extent of drug use in the offender population and on the relationship between drug use and crime.

iii)   The twice-yearly Pulse Check reports on national trends in illicit drug use and markets issued by the White House Office of National Drug Control Policy. These are based on information from a variety of people working in the drugs field and aim to provide timely information about changes and trends as they develop.

49   We recommend that the Government study the United States and Dutch systems with a view to establishing an early warning system in this country that:

i)   comes under the responsibility of a single national body;

ii)   collects and collates information speedily from the relevant national and local agencies, including the police, health services, drug advisory and treatment agencies, and the Drug Action Teams;

iii)   incorporates a network of local and regional bodies responsible for identifying emerging trends in drug use in their areas and for reporting them to the national body. This role might well be performed by the Drug Action Teams.

We recognise that a start has been made in the new arrangements for drug testing of persons arrested by the police. But we do not believe that an early warning system that relies solely or mainly on information about drug use among offenders can be comprehensive or fully effective. And there remains the need to bring information from a variety of sources under one central body.

Chapter Four: Trafficking Offences

Introduction

1   Trafficking is a broad term used to describe the illicit trade in drugs. The Misuse of Drugs Act 1971 (MDA) does not itself distinguish between trafficking and non-trafficking offences. The distinction was made later in legislation introduced in 1986. This is now consolidated in the Drug Trafficking Act 1994. The main relevance of designating an offence as a drug trafficking offence is that conviction will attract the confiscation provisions of that Act. Also, if a Class A drug is involved, a third consecutive conviction for a trafficking offence will result in a minimum sentence of seven years custody under the Crime (Sentences) Act 1997.

2   In our discussion of individual offences in this and the following chapter we adhere to this distinction between trafficking and non-trafficking. It is, however, often blurred in practice. For example, although trafficking offences attract high maximum penalties, they are often used to prosecute rather low-level crimes (for example cultivation of a small number of cannabis plants for personal use). Or they may not be prosecuted at all, as in the case of the many cannabis importation cases dealt with by compounding.

3   Trafficking offenders represent:

(a) 16% of all those found guilty, cautioned, given a fiscal fine or dealt with by compounding for drugs offences in the United Kingdom in 1997

(b) 27% of the total found guilty of drugs offences in all courts

(c) 75% of those found guilty of drugs offences in the higher courts.

It must be borne in mind that the resources needed to detect and prosecute trafficking offences are far higher than for possession offences. The small proportion that they represent of the total of cases dealt with does not necessarily mean that the police and customs fail to give them priority.

What are trafficking offences ?

4   The MDA offences that are trafficking offences for the purpose of the 1994 Act are:

(a) production, supply and possession with intent to supply under section 4 (2) or (3) or 5 (3);

(b) incitement to commit such offences under section 19;

(c) assisting in or inducing the commission outside the United Kingdom of an offence punishable under a corresponding law (section 20).

Cultivation of cannabis under section 6 of the MDA is not a trafficking offence. But since 1982 people found growing cannabis plants are now normally prosecuted for production under section 4 (2), which is. Offences against section 8 (permitting certain activities to take place on premises) are also not drug trafficking offences.

5 A variety of offences under related legislation are also trafficking offences. These include: the offences of improper importation, exportation and fraudulent evasion under the Customs and Excise Management Act 1979 (CEMA); various offences relating to money laundering and the manufacture or supply of particular precursor chemicals to be intentionally used in or for the unlawful production of any controlled drug; and offences of conspiracy and attempt to commit any of the trafficking offences.

The 1988 United Nations Convention

6 As its title makes clear, the United Nations Convention against Illicit Traffic in Narcotic Drugs and Psychotropic Substances, although it considers the problem as a whole[1], is directed specifically against illicit traffic. Accordingly one of the basic features of the convention is the mandatory requirement that the specific activities that constitute or contribute to trafficking be made criminal offences in the law of the parties and those offences must be subject to sanctions which take into account the grave nature of the offences, such as imprisonment or other forms of deprivation of liberty, pecuniary sanctions and confiscation. Measures such as treatment, education, aftercare, rehabilitation or social reintegration may be provided but only in addition to, not instead of, such sanctions.

7 There is, however, an exception for appropriate cases of a minor nature. Where these are concerned, non-punitive sanctions may be used as alternatives, not in addition, to penal sanctions. The convention appears therefore to recognise a category of minor trafficking offence where it may be appropriate to use alternatives[2] to conviction and punishment. The convention also reserves the drafting of the offences to the domestic law of individual countries and provides that offences shall be prosecuted and punished in conformity with that law. The convention therefore allows some room for manoeuvre albeit far less than for non-trafficking offences.

Penalties

8 The maximum penalties, graded according to the Class of drug involved, are the same for all the MDA trafficking offences except those against section 20. (See Table 4.1).

Import/export

9 Importation and exportation are prohibited under section 3 of the MDA unless there is an exception under regulations made under section 7 or a licence from the Secretary of State. But the MDA contains no specific offence of contravening that prohibition. There is in fact no offence of drug-smuggling as such in any Act. The relevant offences are contained in and prosecuted under CEMA, under which it is an offence to import or export anything which is prohibited under any enactment, including the MDA.

---

[1]See paragraph 15 of Preamble to the Convention.
[2]Paragraph 3.108 of the Official Commentary states:'...bridges between the criminal justice system and the treatment system might...be envisaged at...the prosecution stage (for example, conditional discontinuation of criminal proceedings under condition of attending a treatment programme; treatment order pronounced by a prosecuting magistrate in France) or at the stage of enforcement of a prison sentence (transfer from prison to a treatment institution or therapeutic community in certain circumstances.)'

Table 4.1 Maximum penalties for trafficking offences

Offence	Mode of Trial	Class A	Class B	Class C
Importation Production Supply	(a) summary	Six months or a fine of £5,000 or both	Six months or a fine of £5,000 or both	Three months or a fine of £2,500 or both
Possession with Intent to supply Incitement	(b) on indictment	Life or an unlimited fine or both	14 years or an unlimited fine or both	5 years or an unliminted fine or both
Secion 20[1]	(a) summary			6 months or fine of £5,000 or both
	(b) on indictment			14 years, unlimited fine or both

Note: 1. Assisting in or inducing the commission outside the United Kingdom of an offence punishable under a corresponding law. The maximum penalty applies irrespective of the Class of the drug involved.

10   The offence of improper importation is set out in section 50 of CEMA and of exportation in section 68. Section 170 of CEMA creates further offences as follows:

(a)   knowingly acquiring goods subject to a prohibition on importation or exportation (section 170 (1) (a));

(b)   being knowingly concerned in various activities designed to evade such a prohibition (section 170 (1) (b); and

(c)   being in any way knowingly concerned in fraudulent evasion of such a prohibition (section 170 (2)).

The provision most commonly used by H.M. Customs and Excise to prosecute offences is section 170 (2) because it is the most widely drawn offence.

11   Offences under CEMA are almost invariably charged and prosecuted by H.M. Customs and Excise, not by the police and Crown Prosecution Service. If the police wish to bring charges under CEMA they need to obtain an order from the Commissioners of Customs and Excise under section 145. The Association of Chief Police Officers of England, Wales and Northern Ireland (ACPO), in their evidence to us, suggested that there should be a separate offence in the MDA and that all the drugs offences should be consolidated into one Act. The intended result would be that all importation and exportation offences would be prosecuted under the MDA and it would be immaterial which law enforcement agency was involved in the investigation.

12   We were assured by H.M. Customs and Excise that where it is appropriate for the police to prosecute importation offences the need for them to proceed under CEMA presents no practical difficulties. We doubt, however, whether the police often prosecute under CEMA (there appear to be no statistics). It may therefore happen that, in cases displaying similar sets of circumstances, H.M. Customs and Excise will prosecute for a CEMA offence whereas the police will refer their cases to the Crown Prosecution Service for prosecution of an offence under the MDA – probably possession with intent to supply or, in cases where two or more persons are involved, conspiracy to supply the controlled drug.

13   A number of offences under the MDA (e.g. supply, possession, and production) are subject to section 28 of that Act. This provides defences relating to the extent of the defendant's knowledge of facts necessary for the prosecution to prove e.g. that the substance involved was in fact a controlled drug. But section 28 does not apply to CEMA offences. The probable reason for this is that the definition of an offence committed contrary to CEMA implies something about the state of mind of the accused at the moment he committed the offence. The offences of importation and exportation have to be committed with intent to evade duty or a prohibition on importation or exportation. The offence under section 170 (2) is being *knowingly* concerned in the fraudulent evasion of the prohibition. But the upshot is that two cases, on identical facts, can lead to two different results depending on whether the accused is charged under the MDA or CEMA. This is because, under section 28 of the MDA, the burden is on the accused to prove (on a balance of probabilities) that he neither believed, nor suspected, nor had reason

to suspect, that he was handling a controlled drug of some description. By contrast an offence under section 170 (2) of CEMA requires the prosecution to prove that the accused (a) knew that he was concerned in a smuggling venture and (b) he knew that he was smuggling goods of a description which was banned from importation.

Import and export offences under CEMA: the main facts

1,741 people were dealt with for import or export offences in 1997. This represents a fall of 30% since 1990, when the equivalent figure was 2,478. The drug involved was most commonly cannabis (1,189 offenders or 68% of the total). Other drugs concerned were cocaine (417 offenders), heroin (45), amphetamines (36), and ecstasy-type (49). The percentage of cases dealt with by compounding[1] has declined recently from 48% in 1990 to 31% in 1997.

There has been a steady rise in the proportion of those found guilty by the courts who were sentenced to immediate custody from 60% (777 persons) in 1990 to 79% (940 persons) in 1997. The average sentence length of just over $5^1/_2$ years was longer than for any other trafficking offence. The proportion sentenced to over seven years rose from 20% in 1990 to 37% in 1997.

The amount of herbal cannabis and cannabis resin seized by HM Customs rose from 24.9 tonnes in 1990 to 76.9 tonnes in 1997. The amount of seized heroin rose from 576kg to 1,747 kg; of cocaine from 561kg to 2,073 kg. In 1990 36,000 doses of ecstasy were seized and almost one and a half million doses of ecstasy-type drugs in 1997.

Note: 1. A monetary penalty offered to the offender in lieu of prosecution in cases involving amounts of cannabis of 10 grams or less intended for personal used.

Our conclusions on import/export offences

14   We do not regard the present fragmentation of the law between two Acts, the MDA and CEMA, as satisfactory. It has been suggested to us, though we have received no specific evidence on the matter, that it makes cooperation between the police and the customs more difficult than is necessary or desirable. The police can hardly be encouraged to bring prosecutions for smuggling offences under CEMA by the requirement to seek the permission of the Commissioners for Customs and Excise first. Moreover, it is confusing and potentially unjust to have different offences and defences available under the different Acts even though the circumstances may well be much the same and all that differs is the enforcement agency and the statute under which the accused is charged.

15   Ideally we should have liked to begin with a clean sheet and devise a more consistent and logical framework. That might have enabled us to meet the wish of ACPO and the National Crime Squad to see a drug smuggling offence in the MDA. However, such a result might affect the powers currently available to H.M. Customs and Excise in ways neither foreseen nor intended. Reluctantly we have concluded that it would be impracticable within the constraints of time and of resources upon us to devise a workable alternative to the present regime. We cannot be sure that any recommendations we might make would not have an unacceptable impact elsewhere, particularly on the operation of CEMA. Both areas of the law (drugs and importation) are complex and the present system at least

ensures that they interlock in the area of drugs without making either set of laws unworkable. However, because the separation of statutes and enforcement agencies is unsatisfactory and confusing, we recommend that the Government set up a detailed and in-depth examination of this area.

Production

16   Under section 4 (2) or (3) of the MDA it is an offence to produce or to be concerned in the production of a controlled drug unless there is some exception in the regulations made under section 7. 'Produce' is defined in section 37 (1) as meaning, in reference to controlled drugs, producing by manufacture, cultivation or any other method and 'production' has a corresponding meaning. The offence covers a broad range of activities, from small-scale manufacture in home laboratories to factory scale production of synthetic drugs. It can also embrace very low-level acts of production for personal consumption. Acts of conversion or modification of drugs for the purpose of facilitating self-administration are caught by this definition. Thus adding citric acid to base heroin to make it injectable is production, and pharmacists who sell citric acid to addicts might be vulnerable to accusations that they were aiding and abetting, or inciting the offence under section 19. Converting cocaine salt into crack by adding bicarbonate of soda is also production. So is stripping cannabis leaves from the stalk.

17   Cultivation of any kind and on any scale is also production. It may take the form of a few home grown plants in pots or commercial growth in greenhouses or fields. All are covered by the same offence. As already noted, cultivation of cannabis contrary to section 6 of the MDA is not a trafficking offence, although an offence of producing cannabis under section 4 is. This is not a mere technicality because conviction for an offence under section 4 may be followed by confiscation of assets under the Drug Trafficking Act 1994, which does not apply to offences under section 6.

18   The numbers of production offenders are dominated by those dealt with for growing cannabis. The figures do not distinguish cases on the basis of the numbers of plants involved. The number of offenders has fallen in recent years although the proportion given custodial sentences has risen. The proportion receiving one year or less has been stable. The use of cautioning for this offence has fallen but remains significant.

Production offences: the main facts

4,168 persons were dealt with for production offences in 1997. This represents a rise of 663% since 1990, when the equivalent figure was 629. In 1997, 92% or 3,828 had committed offences involving the production of cannabis. Between 1990 and 1997 over 90% have been dealt with for production of cannabis. In 1990, 12% of offenders were cautioned and 25% in 1997.

The proportion of those found guilty who were sentenced to immediate custody more than doubled between 1990 and 1997; 559 or 18% were given such sentences in 1997. The average sentence length was just over 14 months in 1997, the shortest for any trafficking offence. Only 3% received more than 5 years in 1997.

Our conclusions on production

19   We make no recommendations on the various definitional problems that have concerned the courts in the past and may do so again. Our main concern lies in the wide scope of the offence and in particular its embracing all forms of cannabis cultivation from the small domestic to the large-scale commercial. This seems to have been arrived at almost by accident. The original purpose of the MDA was quite clearly to deal with cannabis cultivation under section 6, which creates the specific offence of cultivation of cannabis. A change in the law in 1977 meant that cultivation of cannabis in almost all its forms came under the definition of production. This does not seem to us sufficient reason for all cases of cannabis cultivation to be treated as production offences, especially when section 6 remains on the statute book. The subsequent enactment of the drug trafficking legislation has exposed people who grow a few plants for their own use to the full weight of the confiscation machinery. They stand to lose their assets, including their homes. This seems to us disproportionate even if in practice the law is unlikely to be applied in such cases.

20   We recommend elsewhere[3] that a distinction, implicit in the 1988 United Nations convention, be drawn between more and less serious cases of cultivation of cannabis. The less serious cases, involving small numbers of plants for personal use, would be prosecuted under an amended section 6, which as now would not be a trafficking offence. The more serious offences, particularly of large-scale commercial growing where confiscation of proceeds might well be appropriate, would continue to be prosecuted as production offences under section 4.

Supply

21   Under section 4 (3) it is an offence, unless there is a relevant exception under the regulations made under section 7, to supply a controlled drug to another. It is also an offence to offer to supply, or to be concerned in supply or in making an offer to supply. Under section 37 (1) 'supplying' includes distributing but is not otherwise defined.

22   Difficult issues have been considered by the courts as to what does or does not constitute supply. Existing law has defined supply as including a transfer of physical control of a controlled drug to another with the intention of enabling the recipient to use that drug for his own purposes. Thus

  (a)   to hand drugs to another for safe keeping would not be supply, since the intention is not that the recipient should use them for his own purposes but that he should give them back at a later stage; and

  (b)   the supplier does not have to make a profit or obtain any reward from the transaction for it to constitute the offence of supply. Thus a person who buys drugs and distributes them to friends for consumption at a party is guilty of supply even if he makes no attempt to recover from his friends the money he originally paid for the drugs. Even handing round a reefer from person to person would probably be supply for the purposes of the MDA.

---

[3]See Chapter Seven, paragraph 40.

Supply offences: the main facts

5,864 offenders were dealt with for supply offences in 1997. This represents a rise of 273% since 1990, when the equivalent figure was 2,151. The drugs involved in 1997 included cocaine and crack (323 offenders), heroin (1,040), methadone (85), LSD (64), ecstasy-type (479), amphetamines (916) and cannabis (2,853 or 49%). In 1997, 17 people were cautioned for supplying cocaine, 31 for heroin, 10 for ecstasy, 45 for amphetamines and 390 for cannabis (this was 14% of those dealt with for supply of cannabis).

Of those found guilty by the courts the proportion sentenced to immediate custody rose from 41% (823 persons) in 1990 to 58% (3,084 persons) in 1997. The average length of prison sentence was nearly two and a half years in 1997 with 57% of the sentences for more than one year.

---

23   Other European countries have differentiated in their law between the different kinds of supply, most commonly by providing for aggravating factors that characterise the most serious forms. In Italy, gifts and free exchanges of drugs are categorised as possession for personal use and are subject to administrative sanctions only. So is acquisition, including purchase of drugs by some members of a group on behalf of the group, provided the purchasers are also consumers and that the distributor is not in fact retailing. Purchase by one member on behalf of the whole group is thus a penal offence on the grounds that a transfer or retailing rather than sharing is involved and there is more risk of that transfer leading to the spread of drug consumption.

24   In Spain, gifts of drugs and obtaining them for group use may or may not be an offence depending on the circumstances. The trend of recent legal developments has been to regard these activities as falling outside the range of trafficking if they lead to no risk of dissemination of drugs to people not dependent on them. Thus common funds set up by addicts for the purchase of drugs have been declared as not a matter for prosecution.

Our conclusions on supply

25   The present offence of supply does not distinguish adequately or satisfactorily between circumstances that would ordinarily be regarded as supplying and those that would not. It catches some activities which it is highly misleading to regard as 'trafficking' in any serious sense or at all. These problems arise because the activities of possession and supply so often go together and the boundary between the two is blurred. Small-scale consumption among friends may well involve supply and indeed supply for gain but despite the fact that each member of the group shares a common objective, it is usually the member of the group who actually purchases the drug on behalf of the others who is liable to prosecution. On the other hand, someone who makes it his living and his business to traffic in drugs cannot be charged with just one offence that embraces a course of conduct (e.g. repeated acts of supply, perhaps over weeks or months).

26   Equating these very different circumstances seems to us to confuse some very serious issues. The current definition of supply does not distinguish between acts of

different gravity e.g. supply between friends, or for gain, or as part of an organised criminal group supplying in substantial quantities. We recognise the difficulty of defining 'supply' in terms which will embrace situations that should be punished under section 4 (3) but which allow other situations to escape the scope of that provision. Nevertheless the attempt should be made. It brings the law into disrepute if someone in a social group who acquires drugs on behalf of the rest is taken to be a supplier for the purposes of the law. The context is very different. To meet these difficulties we make the following recommendations.

27 There should be a separate offence of dealing, the main ingredient of which would be the pattern of activity of illicitly transacting business in drugs. The offence should be capable of being charged as a continuing offence so that the prosecution can show that the defendant has been dealing over a period of time by putting before the court evidence of the true scope and nature of his activities. This used to be possible under the present law by alleging sample or specimen counts but changes made by successive Criminal Justice Acts in 1991 and 1993 have made it difficult for the courts to sentence for more than isolated acts of supply. Although such an act may have been part of a continuing pattern of behaviour, the court must sentence the defendant on the basis of what has been proved against him by counts on the indictment or admitted by him.

28 We recognise that the position can to some extent be ameliorated by the prosecution placing two or more single charges on the indictment to the extent necessary to bring out the regular pattern of offending that exists. It may also be possible to allege a conspiracy if two or more persons were involved in supplying the drugs. There may, however, be difficulties about overloading indictments; in any case the offences are still technically separate and establishing the true extent of a defendant's criminal activity over a given period of time may be difficult if not impossible. We therefore recommend a separate offence of dealing as the best way of overcoming the difficulties. We further recommend that the new offence be designated a trafficking offence for the purposes of the Drug Trafficking Act 1994.

29 Those whose acts of supply (or possession with intent to supply) do not involve Class A drugs and are more akin to joint possession for personal use should be enabled to enter a defence that takes them out of the ambit of trafficking offences. They would remain liable to proceedings against them for possession (and indeed for trafficking offences if the drug were one in Class A).

30 We do not recommend that there should be no response at all from the criminal law to acts of group supply. Far from it, since for most people they will be the means of first introducing them to drugs. But the behaviour is different from dealing and the law should recognise the distinction. We recommend accordingly that it should be a defence for a person accused of supply or possession with intent to supply to prove that he was a member of a small social group who supplied or intended to supply a controlled drug (other than a drug of Class A) to another member or other members of that group believing that he was acting, or had acted, on behalf of the group, which shared a common intention to use the drug for personal consumption. This defence would only apply where the court was

satisfied that the amount or value of the controlled drug was consistent with personal use within the group concerned.

31   We recognise that we may be accused of inconsistency in excluding users of Class A drugs from the new defence. In fact we are adhering to the principle that the law on drugs should reflect the relative dangerousness of the drug concerned. Class A drugs may be so damaging that their supply even in a social context must be discouraged to the maximum extent possible. We think it right that those prepared to pass Class A drugs on to others should know that, whatever the context, they face the severest penalties that the law lays down.

Possession with intent to supply

32   Under section 5 (3) of the MDA it is an offence for a person to have a controlled drug in his possession, whether lawfully or not, with intent to supply it to another in contravention of section 4 (1) (which makes it unlawful to supply or offer to supply a controlled drug unless there is an exception of some kind under regulations). The prosecution must prove that the accused was in possession of drugs; that those drugs were controlled drugs; and that he intended to supply them to another.

33   According to section 37 (3), for the purposes of the MDA the things which a person has in his possession shall be taken to include any thing subject to his control which is in the custody of another. Therefore someone who leaves drugs with someone else while looking for likely customers will have no defence against a charge of possession with intent to supply. In practice, intent is proved by quantities incompatible with personal consumption, together with any indications of dealing such as records of transactions or unexplained amounts of money. The offence enables action to be taken against people discovered with large amounts of drugs on them but not in the act of supplying them to others.

34   The pattern of responses to offences of possession with intent to supply is close to that for offences of supply. They can thus be seen as complementing each other, the police and courts seeing possession with intent as containing all the features of a supply offence except the act of supply itself. The number of offenders is greater than the numbers of supply offenders, probably because the act of supply does not need to be proved.

> ### Possession with intent to supply: the main facts
>
> 8,228 persons were dealt with in 1997. This represents a rise of 300% since 1990, when the equivalent was 2,751. The drugs involved in 1997 included cocaine and crack (504 offenders), heroin (1,033), methadone (30), LSD (132), ecstasy-type (843), amphetamines (1,672) and cannabis (4,476 or 54% of all offenders). 6% of offenders were cautioned; the proportion of cannabis offenders cautioned was 8%.
>
> The proportion of those found guilty by the courts who were sentenced to immediate custody rose from 41% (1,114 persons) in 1990 to 57% (4,404 persons) in 1997. The average sentence length in 1997 was just under two years. 50% were given sentences of over one year.

Our conclusions on possession with intent to supply

35 We make no recommendations on the specific offence of possession with intent to supply. If it were not there, it would be possible for people found with large amounts of drugs in circumstances that clearly indicated supply to avoid severe punishment on the grounds that no actual transfer of the drugs could be proved. It is therefore a useful aspect of United Kingdom legislation, not found as far as we know elsewhere, and gives added strength to the law's armoury against supply. The offence should therefore be retained, though it should attract the new defence that we recommend at paragraph 30 above.

Our recommendations on maximum penalties for trafficking offences

36 The maximum penalties for trafficking offences laid down in the MDA and related legislation are among the most severe in Europe. A (necessarily rough) comparison of United Kingdom maximum penalties for trafficking offences with those in five other European countries is given in the following table. As can be seen, the United Kingdom is particularly out of line in its maximum penalty for trafficking in cannabis, largely because of its classification as a Class B drug.

Table 4.2 Maximum penalties for trafficking offences in EU states

Country	Maximum penalty in years (hard drugs)	Maximum penalty in years (soft drugs, including cannabis)
France	30[1] to Life[2]	5[3]
Germany	minimum 1 to maximum 15[4]	5
Italy	30[5]	6
The Netherlands	12[6]	4
Spain	20[7]	3
United Kingdom	Life[8]	5[9]-14[10]

Notes.   1. Involved in organised group trafficking

2. Directing international organised drug trafficking

3. Incitement by small scale trafficking to adult

4. Supplying drugs to minors

5. Aggravated supply of hard drugs

6. Import of hard drugs

7. Supply with 2nd degree aggravating features

8. Trafficking in Class A

9. Trafficking in Class C

10. Trafficking in Class B, which includes cannabis

37   There is a respectable argument for prescribing maximum penalties at a level which allows the courts to reflect in the actual sentences passed the wide range of variation of circumstances likely to be encountered. Nevertheless it seems to us that the maximum penalties on indictment in United Kingdom law are unreasonably high. Life imprisonment is excessive for almost any conceivable drugs offence. Nor are we aware that it has ever been imposed. Thus the discrepancy between maximum penalties and sentences actually passed is so great as to risk bringing the law into disrepute. We therefore prefer a set of penalties that is credible and not disproportionate; that is not out of line with the rest of Europe; still enables the courts to pass severe sentences for the offences at the top end of the scale of seriousness but is not too different from the sentences they normally pass.

38   It is difficult and to some extent arbitrary to devise a scale of maximum penalties which achieves these objectives and still provides a major disincentive to would-be traffickers, especially given the reduction in the maximum penalties for trafficking in cannabis that follow from our recommendation to transfer it to Class C. In fact, we propose below an increase in the maximum penalty for trafficking in Class C drugs to take account of this.

39   It should also be borne in mind that confiscation measures are probably at least as important as fines and imprisonment in deterring trafficking. Failure to meet the requirements of a confiscation order may lead to substantial additional terms of imprisonment in default (of up to ten years depending on the amount involved). Only if such measures are severe and effective will drug traffickers be prevented from realising the profits that may otherwise make a long prison sentence seem a price worth paying. We have taken account of this extra dimension in arriving at our recommended maximum penalties, which we set out in the following table alongside the penalties prescribed in the present law. This table covers only penalties for MDA and CEMA offences. The other drug trafficking offences, such as money laundering and illicit traffic in precursor chemicals, should be separately considered and, if necessary to achieve consistency, their penalties brought into line.

Sentencing guidelines

40   We are satisfied that the maximum penalties recommended above will continue to leave the courts with discretion to sentence subject to the facts of the case. The law will retain the flexibility necessary to enable the courts to respond appropriately to the great variety of circumstances met by them. There are, however, some aggravating circumstances to which we believe the courts should have consistent regard.

41   To assist the courts to achieve these objectives with consistency, we believe that sentencing guidelines should be laid down for drugs cases generally and in particular for drug trafficking offences. Sections 80 and 81 of the Crime and Disorder Act 1998 require the criminal division of the Court of Appeal to consider framing guidelines for offences of the relevant category and in doing so to have

Table 4.3   Maximum penalties on indictment[1] for trafficking offences: our recommendations compared to present law

Importation, production, supply, possession with intent to supply

Class A now	Class A new	Class B now	Class B new	Class C now	Class C new
Life or an unlimited fine or both	20 years or an unlimited fine or both	14 years or an unlimited fine or both	no change	5 years or an unlimited fine or both	7 years or an unlimited fine or both

New offence of dealing

As for our recommendations for importation, production, supply, and possession with intent to supply.

Section 20[2]

14 years or an unlimited fine or both

Incitement

At present the maximum penalties for incitement are the same as for the offences incited. We recommend no change.

Notes: 1. We are not recommending any change to the present maximum penalties on summary conviction.

2. Assisting in or inducing the commission outside the United Kingdom of an offence punishable under a corresponding law. The Class of the drug involved is not relevant.

regard to the views of the Sentencing Advisory Panel. We recommend that drugs offences be designated as a relevant category of offences and that guidelines be proposed by the Panel for consideration by the Court of Appeal.

42   We do not wish to pre-empt the work of the Sentencing Advisory Panel or the Court of Appeal. We do, however, wish to indicate the aggravating factors that should be included in the guidelines when they are drawn up. Some of these are so important that we have considered creating separate offences to ensure that the seriousness of certain situations is properly reflected in the sentences handed down. We have particularly in mind the supply of drugs to children and young persons, the employment of minors in drug trafficking, the introduction of drugs into schools, prisons and psychiatric facilities, and the creation of public nuisance through drugs activities.

43   On balance we have concluded that the better approach is to retain the present fairly broad formulation of individual offences, leaving their application in particular contexts to the discretion, subject to guidelines, of the courts. We recommend that among the factors to be taken account of in such guidelines should be:

i)   the involvement in the offence of an organised criminal group to which the defendant belongs;

ii)   the use of violence or firearms by the defendant;

iii) whether drugs were supplied to children or young persons;

iv)   whether children or young persons were employed to assist in the commission of the offence or related offences;

v)   whether the offence took place on or in the vicinity of schools, psychiatric facilities, prisons or any other institution or facility designed to meet the needs of the young or vulnerable;

vi)   whether the commission of the offence was, or contributed to, a public nuisance over and above the ingredients of the offence itself (e.g. if committed in a public place to the annoyance or intimidation of members of the public other than the offender and his victim).

Confiscation

44   Confiscation is important for several reasons. First, it is a recognised and established principle that offenders should not benefit from their crimes – an effective confiscatory mechanism ensures this. Second, by stripping the offender of the proceeds of his criminal activities in addition to any other penalty, it provides a major deterrent to further crime by him and others. Third, it prevents the proceeds of organised crime from being reinvested so that, even if the penalty of the law falls on a subordinate (for example, a courier) or a middleman, the main organisers may still be frustrated by being deprived of any proceeds. The life blood of drug trafficking is cash flow, and the aim of the confiscation legislation which we fully support is, by extracting tainted property from offenders, to prevent their reinvestment in further drug trafficking or other forms of criminal activity.

45   An important feature of trafficking offences is that conviction may be followed by orders for confiscation of assets under the Drug Trafficking Act 1994. Under this Act the court is required to assume that any property held by the defendant at the time of his conviction or transferred to him at any time in the previous six years is payment or reward for drug trafficking unless that assumption is disproved by the defendant or there would be a serious risk of injustice in allowing it to stand. The standard of proof that applies is the civil one of the balance of probabilities and not the criminal law standard of beyond reasonable doubt.

46   The following other main features of the 1994 Act may be noted:
   i)   What is to be confiscated are the proceeds not the profits of the trafficking. Thus the offender cannot deduct expenses incurred as part of his drug trafficking activities.
   ii)   It is irrelevant whether the trafficking took place in the United Kingdom or abroad.
   iii) Special provisions apply enabling confiscation to proceed despite the death or absconding of the accused .
   iv)   Various offences are created, including concealing, disguising, transferring or removing the proceeds of drug trafficking.
   v)   Gifts made by the defendant may be included in the amount ordered by the court to be recovered. So, for example, money given to a wife or husband towards the purchase of a house may lead to confiscation of that part of the house's value judged to stem from the gift.
   vi)   Enforcement of confiscation orders is either through the magistrates' courts fine enforcement machinery or through the appointment by the High Court of a receiver with powers to seize, realise and manage the defendant's assets.
   vii) Under Part II of the Act, a customs or police officer can seize money being imported or exported where there are reasonable grounds to suspect that it is connected to drug trafficking. For the purposes of Part II such cash can be forfeited and condemned without any conviction for a drug trafficking offence in connection with the money.

47   The evidence strongly suggests that the present system is not as effective as it should be. The number of confiscation orders rose steadily from 203 in 1987 to over 1,000 in 1991. In 1995 they reached a peak of 1,562 but in 1997 there was a 6% fall to 1,466. More significantly the total amount ordered to be confiscated almost halved in 1997 as compared to 1996, from £10.5 million to £5.6 million. This is the lowest figure since 1991. The average amount ordered to be confiscated also fell in 1997, by over a half from £6,725 in 1996 to £3,834. This is the lowest ever amount. Seizures by customs or police officers of money being imported or exported took place in 619 cases in 1997 although the cash was returned in the great majority of them. £2.9 million was ordered to be forfeited by the courts.

48   Professor Michael Levi has prepared for us an assessment of the effectiveness of the present law which more than confirms our impression that it is not being implemented well. As he says in his report 'Administration of confiscation orders remains a mess, inasmuch as magistrates' courts are not the ideal body for dealing with devious, high level international manipulations...' He notes also that when

confiscation actually occurs, the values are usually substantially less than the value of the amount initially frozen because, among other reasons, some assets presumed to exist cannot be found or because it is not possible to convince a judge that there was really any link between the assets and the crime. He goes on to say 'When assessing the overall effect of asset confiscation, the stark gap between guesstimates of money-laundering volumes and confiscation orders made, let alone actual confiscation effected, is evident...'.

49 Professor Levi observes that during the 1990s the sums confiscated in up to half the cases in which orders were made were of £1,000 or less, which suggests either that few top traffickers are convicted or that, where they are convicted, few realisable assets can be found. It is this sort of frustration that gives impetus to the recommendations of the recent Home Office consultation paper[4].

50 The Home Office consultation paper contains a package of no less than 18 measures designed to improve the enforcement of confiscation orders. A further five recommendations are made for strengthening the existing law in other ways. In addition, the working group proposes a civil law procedure, in connection with which it makes a further 15 recommendations. Under this procedure confiscation would be sought of the assets of persons who have not been convicted of an offence but whose assets can be shown on the balance of probabilities to have come from drug trafficking. The working group suggests that a new national confiscation agency be considered with the remit of overseeing the new civil forfeiture system, of enforcing confiscation orders made by the higher courts under the existing criminal law system, and assisting other agencies in seeking confiscation orders in major cases.

51 We doubt whether the case has been made out for confiscation of assets under civil law procedure, at least at this stage. Such provisions are already part of the law in the United States and the Republic of Ireland. They may be a useful source of financing law enforcement services but this aspect has attracted criticism in the United States from a former Attorney General[5] among others on the grounds that it sets up a conflict of interest between 'economic self-interest and traditional law enforcement objectives'.

52 The long-term effect of such measures on drug trafficking is less well proven. Indeed it is a complaint frequently made by commentators that the United States system actually benefits drugs trade organisers, who can buy their freedom through the civil confiscation machinery while subordinate suppliers bear the full brunt of the criminal law. Our fundamental objection, however, is that so radical a departure needs more justification than the disappointing results shown so far in operating the present criminal law system. We therefore take the view that the first priority is to strengthen and make maximum use of the existing criminal law procedures.

53 At present, except where a receiver is appointed by the High Court, the magistrates' courts are responsible for recovering the assets named in a confiscation order. They may find themselves called upon to enforce an order in an amount of several million pounds with a default term of up to ten years. These are amounts

---

[4]Home Office Working Group on Confiscation, *Third Report: Criminal Assets,* November 1998.
[5]Richard Thornburgh, quoted in E. Blumenson and E. Nilsen, 'Contesting government's interest in drug cases', *Criminal Justice* (Winter 1999), 4-10, as saying 'it's now possible for a drug dealer to serve time in a forfeiture-financed prison after being arrested by agents driving a forfeiture-provided automobile while working in a forfeiture-funded sting operation.'

and sentences wholly inconsistent with the maximum penalties that a magistrates' court can impose on conviction, and we doubt whether they are the appropriate jurisdiction for the task. We therefore recommend that the responsibility for enforcement should lie with the crown court not with the magistrates' courts. This will enable the same court as made the order, and often the same judge, to oversee its implementation, including referring it in suitable cases to the High Court for the appointment of a receiver.

54   As far as time to pay is concerned, the Home Office consultation paper suggests that the courts should be required to order either immediate payment or payment within six months. We think that this is insufficiently flexible. We agree that a time limit for payment should be set and that it should not be possible to leave this open as at present. But the limit set should be that which seems reasonable to the court having looked into the circumstances and heard and tested the arguments of prosecution and defence. There may be circumstances where the realisation of assets is likely to take longer than six months.

55   Subject to our recommendation to transfer all enforcement responsibility to the higher courts, and to our proposals on time limits for payment, we endorse the recommendations in the Home Office consultation paper for improving the effectiveness of the present system. Several of those recommendations would, however, be overtaken by our recommendations because the consultation paper envisages enforcement responsibilities remaining with the magistrates' courts. Many of the recommendations in the consultation paper are therefore either unnecessary or in need of adaptation to fit the needs of the higher courts.

56   These changes would represent a substantial change to the criminal law and more than justify the setting up of a new national confiscation agency, as recommended by the Home Office working group. The case for the agency does not in our view depend on the introduction of a new civil law procedure. The arguments for that might be reconsidered once the amended criminal law enforcement machinery, overseen by the new agency, has had the opportunity of operating to its full potential for some years. In the meantime, we recommend that the new agency be set up with the overriding remit of ensuring that the present criminal confiscation machinery, reformed as we propose, achieves full efficiency.

57   We stress, however, that if full efficiency is to be achieved a considerable investment in recruitment and training of people with the requisite skills will be needed in most branches of the criminal justice system, in particular the police, prosecution, and courts (including the judges). We sense that at present there is widespread lack of enthusiasm for pursuing confiscation as a response to offending because of the complexity of the law and of the methods that offenders resort to in order to hide away their ill-gotten gains. The police must be adequately resourced and soundly trained in the necessary financial investigative skills to counteract these methods. The prosecution and the courts must equally be made more knowledgeable about the means to be employed to trace assets, and be prepared to direct the efforts of the police where necessary. This is difficult and time-consuming work. The police may be reluctant to divert resources to it unless the

need to give it priority is properly recognised, both by the Government in allocating resources and in the performance indicators set nationally for the police. At present these appear to treat all supply offences equally, thus encouraging the police to go for a greater number of easy targets rather than a smaller number of higher level cases.

Forfeiture

58 Section 27 of the MDA enables the court to order the forfeiture of anything shown to be related to the offence of which the defendant has been convicted. It applies to all MDA offences, not only the trafficking ones. It is far more narrowly drawn than the confiscation powers under the Drug Trafficking Act 1994. It may nevertheless be useful in minor cases, especially as it is easier to operate than the powers under the 1994 Act. We have been told that its implementation would be improved if the following changes are made:

a) extension of the section to apply to houses, land and other real property, which the courts have decided are outside its scope;

b) its extension to overseas property, whether within the jurisdiction of the United Kingdom courts or not;

c) its extension to cover property shown to the court's satisfaction to relate to other drug trafficking or intended to be used in connection with such trafficking;

d) amendment of the section in order to clarify its relationship to section 43 of the Powers of Criminal Courts Act 1973.

59 We agree that it should be possible for the courts to order the forfeiture of property other than land seized by the police which was clearly about to be used in the commission of a further offence (the second limb of paragraph 58 (c) above). We are not in favour of amending the section in other ways since that seems to us to risk overelaboration in what is a relatively straightforward area, suitable for simpler cases that do not require the full weight of the confiscation machinery. To go further risks duplication of and confusion with that machinery.

Precursors

60 Part II of the Criminal Justice (International Co-operation) Act 1990 was passed to enable the United Kingdom to meet its obligations under the 1988 United Nations Convention. The Act lists the main chemicals (known as precursors) that can be used to manufacture illicit drugs. These are subject to various controls designed to minimise the risk of their being obtained by criminals. Manufacture or supply of the listed precursors knowing or suspecting that they are to be used in or for the unlawful production of a controlled drug is, under section 12, a trafficking offence for the purpose of the Drug Trafficking Act 1994. Section 13 enables regulations to be made governing notification of exports, record keeping and the supply of information. It is an offence to fail to comply with the regulations or to give false information in an attempt to comply with them. In addition, there exists a voluntary scheme by which companies are encouraged to cooperate with the

police and to notify them of requests for the supply of chemicals that may be used in the production of controlled drugs.

61   We have considered proposals put to us for strengthening this machinery. These are essentially directed at putting the present voluntary scheme on a statutory and compulsory basis. This would entail adding to the number of chemicals listed as precursors in the 1990 Act and requiring companies to notify the police of all orders for them above specified levels. We can see the force of this suggestion in principle but do not believe that it would be effective in practice. There are innumerable chemicals which may be used in drug production and most if not all of them have legitimate uses. The police would therefore be likely to be swamped with meaningless notifications. We are not persuaded that an extension of the law in the direction suggested would work and make no recommendation on the matter.

Chapter Five: Non-Trafficking Offences

Introduction: relevance of United Nations conventions

1   In this chapter we discuss the remaining offences created by the MDA where these raise important issues. But we defer discussion of section 6 (cultivation of cannabis) to Chapter Seven.

2   Possession is the key issue. The United Nations conventions permit more latitude in this area than with trafficking offences. Parties are required under article 3, paragraph 2, of the 1988 convention to establish possession for personal consumption as a criminal offence under their domestic law. This requirement, unlike that for trafficking offences, is subject to a country's 'constitutional principles and the basic concepts of its legal system'. This is particularly relevant for those countries whose constitutions enshrine principles of personal freedom, including the freedom to harm oneself.

3   In Italy, possession for personal use is an administrative infringement only; in Spain it is not lawful but it is not an offence unless it occurs in public, when it attracts administrative sanctions only. This results from the application of the constitutional principles of those countries and the basic concepts of their legal systems. It must, however, be borne in mind that the sanctions for administrative offences are not necessarily trivial. In Italy, for example, they may include suspension of one's driving licence, gun licence or passport; in Spain also, driving and gun licenses may be temporarily withdrawn and other sanctions include fines or closure of the premises where the use took place.

4   Drug use as such is not a criminal offence in many countries (nor do the United Nations conventions seem to require this, although the interpretation is disputed). The United Kingdom and Ireland make it an offence to use opium; it is not an offence to use other drugs. In their case it is seen as sufficient to make possession the offence.

5   A crucial contrast between trafficking offences and possession for personal use lies in the sanctions to be provided. Under article 3, paragraph 4 (a), of the 1988 convention, trafficking offences must be punishable by imprisonment or other forms of deprivation of liberty, pecuniary sanctions and confiscation. There is no such requirement for possession for personal consumption. Although there are administrative sanctions for possession for personal use in Italy and Spain, there is no imprisonment. In countries where possession for personal use is a criminal offence, imprisonment is normally among the possible sanctions but this is not a requirement of the United Nations conventions.

6   Whatever the penal sanctions provided, article 3, paragraph 4(d), of the 1988 convention permits measures for the treatment, education, aftercare, rehabilitation or social reintegration of the offender to be provided as alternatives to conviction or punishment. As with trafficking offences, the definition, prosecution and

punishment of personal consumption offences are reserved to the domestic law of the states which are party to the conventions. Accordingly, laws may broadly correspond as between nations but not be identical. Similarly, the parties to the conventions are afforded a greater latitude of discretion over enforcement and punishment than is generally understood.

7   In many cases, therefore, prosecution does not take place or the courts may respond to offences with non-penal measures. In the Netherlands, for example, the application of the expediency principle in the public interest results in the police and prosecution authorities waiving prosecution in most cases of possession of any drug in small quantities for personal use. As far as cannabis is concerned, prosecution is also waived in a wide range of offences involving its sale through coffee shops, in accordance with formal Dutch policy. In Germany, prosecution guidelines in cases of small amounts for personal consumption vary among the 16 Bundeslander, resulting in rates of non-prosecution of between 0.2% and 30.6% for all drugs offences and between 40-50% and 80-90% for cannabis cases. Almost all countries combine treatment provision with the criminal justice process.

Possession

8   Section 5 (1) of the MDA makes it unlawful to have a controlled drug in one's possession unless there is a relevant exemption in regulations under section 7. Subsection (2) makes it an offence to contravene this prohibition. Section 37 (3) states that the things which a person has in his possession shall be taken to include anything subject to his control which is in the custody of another. The offence is not specifically confined to possession for personal use. It covers any offence of possession where intent to supply cannot be proved. In effect personal use cases come under it but it is no defence to claim that the possession was neither for supply nor for use.

9   The defences available under section 28[1] apply to this offence but in addition section 5 (4) provides two special defences. Under the first, it is a defence for the accused to prove that he took possession of the drug for the purpose of preventing someone else from committing an offence in connection with it. He must in addition prove that after taking control of it he took such steps as were reasonably open to him to destroy it or to deliver it to someone lawfully entitled to take custody of it. The second defence is that he took possession of it for the purpose of delivering it into the custody of a person lawfully entitled to take custody of it and that as soon as possible after taking possession he took all such steps as were reasonably open to him to deliver it to such a person. The second defence, unlike the first, is not dependent on taking delivery in order to prevent the commission of a criminal offence: on the other hand it does not allow the drug concerned to be destroyed. In both cases the burden is on the accused to prove the defence.

---

[1]See Chapter One, paragraph 33.

Table 5.1 **Maximum penalties for possession**

Mode of trial	Class A	Class B	Class C
(a) summary	six months or a fine of £5,000 or both	three months or a fine of £2,500 or both	three months or a fine of £1,000 or both
(b) on indictment	seven years or an unlimited fine or both	five years or an unlimited fine or both	two years or an unlimited fine or both

10   The maximum penalties for possession are shown in the preceding box. The Court of Appeal has said that fines are the most appropriate response to the possession of small amounts of cannabis for personal use. Custodial sentences are not ruled out in cases of persistent offending. The evidence we received suggests that custodial sentences are rare for possession of any drug if that is the only offence.

> ### Possession offences: the main facts
>
> 100,808 people (or 89% of all drugs offenders) were dealt with for possession offences in 1997. The numbers have gone up more than two and a half times since 1990 (39,350 persons). 69% (77,943 persons) were found in possession of cannabis. In 1997, 54% of all offenders were cautioned, and 58% of those dealt with for possessing cannabis.
>
> The proportion of those found guilty by the courts who were sentenced to immediate custody was 11% (4,852 persons) in 1997, compared with 3% (1,551 persons) in 1990, more than for any other drugs offence. In 2,843 of these cases, possession was the drugs offence for which the longest sentence was given. Non-drugs offences may well have been involved in addition and/or there may have been earlier drugs convictions. The number sent to prison for a first offence of possession without any other offences being involved is likely to be very small but cannot be determined from the statistics. The average length of a custodial sentence was just under 4 months, the shortest for any drugs offence. 45% of those receiving such sentences were sentenced to one month or less and 96% to one year or less.

Our conclusions

11   The United Nations conventions impose an obligation on the United Kingdom to establish possession for personal consumption as a criminal offence. Even if this were not so, there would be a strong case for creating such an offence, particularly in relation to Class A drugs, given the undeniable existence of problem drug use with consequences that go far beyond the health risk to the individual. We therefore conclude that the offence of possession should remain even where there is no intention to supply and the drug is meant for personal consumption. Nevertheless, the law should be flexible to minimise the harmful consequences of a contravention in appropriate cases. Where problem drug use is not involved, possession alone, even if repeated, should not necessarily result in a conviction. The law should, as the United Nations conventions allow, take full advantage of the leeway left by the conventions to deal with the less serious situations in a less

punitive way. Our recommendations to this end are set out in the following paragraphs.

12   Prison sentences for possession only offences are not commensurate with the harm done by the offence, and they impose substantial harm of their own. If the objective is to reduce individual and social harm, as we believe it must be, there are better responses available whatever the drug involved. As the Advisory Council on the Misuse of Drugs concluded[2] 'drug-related problems are more effectively addressed in the community than in a custodial setting'.

13   But abolishing custodial penalties would rule out some community sanctions that are available to the courts only as alternatives to imprisonment. In most serious cases of problem drug use this will not matter because the offender charged with possession is likely to be charged with other offences at the same time. There may, however, be cases of problem drug users in possession of Class A drugs but not charged with any other offence where the courts need to consider the full range of community orders. Because of the pre-eminent harm of Class A drugs, we accept that a custodial sanction may be needed in such cases. It would act both as an incentive to treatment and in order to enable the courts to consider the use of a wider range of such orders, including community service orders, than would otherwise be possible. For this reason we accept that a maximum penalty of imprisonment albeit on a lower scale than at present should be retained for Class A drugs.

14   In the case of Class B and Class C drugs, we recommend that the present custodial penalties be removed and that the courts develop further the non-custodial responses already available to them (which will in many cases also be appropriate for users of Class A drugs). These responses include fines, probation orders, probation orders with treatment conditions attached, and conditional discharges. We set out our recommendations on fixed out-of-court penalties in Chapter Eight. They are in our opinion particularly suitable for cases of possession of Class B or Class C drugs but only in cases where something more than a caution is needed.

15   We accept that abolishing custodial penalties for possession of Class B and C drugs rules out several other options that would otherwise be available to the courts, but we do not see the necessity to go beyond probation, probation with a condition of treatment, fines or conditional discharges. The courts have developed methods of enforcement that keep imprisonment for non-compliance to a minimum. In cases of possession of Class B and C drugs, fines can be considered for failure to comply with a probation order. It is also possible for the court to impose a community service order as a sanction for breach of a probation order.

16   The Government guidelines on drug treatment and testing orders[3] suggest that they are envisaged as being particularly suitable for those convicted of acquisitive crimes committed in order to obtain money to buy drugs. This leaves open the question of how best to deal with offenders whose only offence is possession of drugs but with whom there are clear indications of problem use of drugs, not necessarily involving drug-related crime. We believe that the test should be whether, at the time they come to the attention of the courts, their drug-taking

---

[2] *Drug Misusers and the Criminal Justice System, Part III: Drug Misusers and the Prison System - an Integrated Approach,* London, HMSO 1996. Paragraph 1.17.
[3] See Chapter Eight, paragraphs 26-28.

includes such features as dependence, regular excessive use and serious health and other social consequences. If it does, the courts have a wide range of sanctions that enable them to choose an appropriate response.

17   Even where Class A drugs are involved, we agree that, as the Home Office guidance suggests, a drug treatment and testing order may not be appropriate for offenders who have been convicted of possession only. There are, however, other disposals not depending on the availability of penalties of imprisonment which the courts can use. It has, in particular, been possible since the Criminal Justice Act 1991 to attach to probation orders conditions that require treatment. The offender's consent is required. Because problem drug use is closely linked with many other problems including unemployment and homelessness, such orders are a constructive approach to tackling this range of issues. There is recent evidence[4] of the effectiveness of such orders in retaining offenders in treatment and reducing their drug use.

18   Drug treatment and testing orders may only be used in areas where the Secretary of State has certified that the necessary facilities are available. When this happens, they can be used concurrently with probation orders but it will no longer be possible to attach treatment conditions to probation orders in drugs cases. Thus the courts in those areas will not be able to use probation orders with treatment conditions attached. This is a retrograde step because it deprives the courts of an appropriate and effective response to minor cases where there is evidence of problem drug use. Although in theory drug treatment and testing orders might be used, it is clear that this is not what they were designed for. Moreover their enforcement through regular drug testing and reports to the courts on progress goes far beyond the requirements of possession only offences. We therefore recommend that, as soon as legislative opportunity permits, the progressive repeal of the ability of the courts to attach treatment conditions to probation orders in drugs cases is reversed.

19   We recommend that the maximum penalties on summary conviction for possession of Class A drugs be six months imprisonment (the same as at present) or a fine of £2,500 (as compared with the present £5,000) or both. For Class B the maximum penalty on summary conviction should be a fine of £1,000 (instead of £2,500 as at present) and for Class C a fine of £500 (instead of £1,000 as at present). On indictment the maximum penalties for possession of Class A drugs should be one year's imprisonment (in place of the present seven years) or an unlimited fine or both. There is no need to set maximum penalties on indictment for possession offences involving drugs in Classes B and C; we do not believe that custody should be available in such cases and accordingly we see no need to try them on indictment at all. They would become offences triable summarily only. The following table sets out our recommendations alongside the present maximum penalties.

---

[4] M. Edmunds, T. May, M. Hough, *Doing Justice to Treatment: referring offenders to drug services*, DPAS Paper 2, London, Home Office 1999.

Table 5.2 Maximum penalties for possession: present law compared to our recommendations

(a) summary

Class A now	Class A new	Class B now	Class B new	Class C now	Class C new
six months or a fine of £5,000 or both	six months or a fine of £2,500 or both	three months or a fine of £2,500 or both	a fine of £1000	three months or a fine of £1,000 or both	a fine of £500

(b) on indictment

Class A now	Class A new	Class B now	Class B new	Class C now	Class C new
seven years or an unlimited fine or both	one year or an unlimited fine or both	five years or an unlimited fine or both	not applicable	two years or an unlimited fine or both	not applicable

Arrestability

20   The powers of arrest in section 24 of the MDA have been replaced in England and Wales by the arrest provisions of the Police and Criminal Evidence Act 1984 (PACE). Section 24 of PACE lays down that any offence for which the maximum penalty on indictment is five years imprisonment or more is an 'arrestable offence'. So are certain offences, listed in section 24 (2) of PACE, that have maximum penalties of less than five years custody. The only conditions that have to be met are that the constable must have reasonable grounds for suspecting that an arrestable offence has been committed and that the person he is about to arrest is guilty of the offence. He may also arrest anyone who is about to commit an arrestable offence or anyone whom he has reasonable grounds for suspecting to be about to commit one.

21   Where the offence is arrestable under section 24 of PACE the police may arrest suspects without a warrant and take them to the police station for further questioning; search premises without a warrant under section 18 of PACE for evidence of the offence for which the arrest was made and any connected and similar offences; and enter premises without a warrant under section 17 of the same Act and search them for the purpose of arresting a person for an arrestable offence. It is these related powers that the police have argued, in evidence to us, are particularly valuable in collecting evidence across a broad front of crime without the offender being able to warn accomplices.

22   Where the offence is not arrestable under section 24 of PACE, police powers are more limited. Under section 25 of PACE suspects may be arrested without warrant only if

      i)   it is impracticable to serve a summons on them or

      ii)   their addresses are unknown or uncertain or

      iii) the arrest is necessary to prevent them from injuring themselves or others, causing damage or obstructing the highway.

23   In Scotland, where PACE does not apply, police officers have powers of detention for up to six hours under section 14 of the Criminal Procedure (Scotland) Act 1995 for any offence punishable by imprisonment. This is not a power of arrest: it enables the police to detain suspects for the purpose of facilitating the carrying out of investigations. In addition section 24 of the MDA remains in force. Under this any person suspected with reasonable cause of committing an offence under the MDA may be arrested if

      i)   the constable believes with reasonable cause that the person will abscond unless arrested or

      ii)   he does not know and cannot ascertain the suspect's name and address or

      iii) he is not satisfied that the name and address supplied is true.

      The maximum penalty is not relevant.

24   Under our recommendations for lower penalties for possession, no possession offence would be arrestable under section 24 of PACE. The maximum penalty for

possessing Class A drugs would be well below the 5 year criterion and there would be no penalty of imprisonment at all for Class B. It should be noted that possession of Class C drugs is not arrestable at present because the maximum penalty is 2 years. We have not been informed of any problems arising from this.

25   In Scotland, police powers of arrest would not change if, as we envisage, section 24 of the MDA continued to apply there. The powers of detention under section 14 of the Criminal Procedure (Scotland) Act 1995 would continue to apply to possession of Class A drugs. They would not, however, apply to possession of Class B drugs since there would no longer be a maximum penalty of imprisonment. Nor would they apply to offences of possession of cannabis, since that would be transferred to Class C and possession offences where Class C drugs are involved do not at present attract section 14 powers.

26   We have considered whether special provision outside PACE should be made to retain the present police powers of arrest in England and Wales. If the effect of arrestability under section 24 of PACE is to be retained in whole or in part in England and Wales, the options are to retain it

i)   for Class A drugs or

ii)   for drugs in both Classes A and B or

iii) for cannabis when it is transferred from Class B to Class C or

iv)   all three of the above.

27   By far the most contentious issue is the powers of arrest that should apply to cannabis possession. As we have argued in Chapter Three, there is no disputing the case on grounds of relative harm for moving this drug from Class B to Class C. The police service have, however, put to us a strong case on pragmatic grounds for retaining their present powers of arrest. They argue that their ability to disrupt illicit drugs markets would be seriously hampered without a power of arrest on the lines of section 24 of PACE. Cannabis is often sold in such markets along with other drugs. The ability to arrest for its possession can often be the first step to arresting people who are dealing in other more serious drugs. This opportunity would be lost if the cannabis offender had to be released and could then warn accomplices and destroy evidence that might otherwise be found in searches conducted under the related powers of PACE. Establishing continuity of evidence from purchaser to dealer would become impossible. Alternative detection techniques (involving for example surveillance or undercover work) can be used. But they are expensive compared to the more economical and equally effective tactic of stopping and searching those attending the market and arresting those on whom cannabis is found while evidence of more serious drugs crimes is collected.

28   The police further argue that even where cannabis markets are isolated from the markets in other drugs their presence is a major nuisance to communities, especially on housing estates, and police powers to deal with them should not be weakened in any way. The police have been given a joint responsibility, with local authorities, for seeking anti-social behaviour orders in appropriate cases under the Crime and Disorder Act 1998. Removing arrestability from cannabis possession

would hamper the contribution they might otherwise be able to make to combating neighbourhood nuisance.

29   The power of arrest for cannabis possession is also, in the police view, invaluable as a means of detecting other more serious offences, and this is not limited to drugs offences. It may lead to arrests for other kinds of offences, for example those involving weapons. An examination of 811 reports of cannabis offences across eight representative divisions of the Metropolitan Police Service suggested that between 2.5% and 10% of cannabis possession cases are linked with other offences. In 1998/99 this might have meant that between 530 and 2,100 cases would have been undetected across the Metropolitan Police District as a whole had possession of cannabis not been an arrestable offence. The actual range may be lower because it is unclear in how many of these cases cannabis possession was the first offence to be detected, and led on to the discovery of more serious offences, and in how many cases cannabis was found at the same time or after the more serious offences were detected.

30   There would also be an increased risk of allegations against police officers that drugs taken from offenders on the streets were being sold on corruptly or otherwise misused. This risk is minimised at present by the application of various procedures for recording and destroying seized drugs but these take place at the police station after arrest. This protection, which benefits suspects as well as police officers, would be greatly reduced if cannabis, overwhelmingly the main drug seized, were transferred to Class C without arrestability being retained.

31   We have much sympathy with these arguments but we have not been persuaded by them. We have considered the results of the examination of cannabis cases described in paragraph 29 but we do not believe that the opportunity costs of removing arrestability for cannabis possession are significant or that the arrest of people in possession of cannabis leads at all frequently to arrests for more serious offences. Indeed, we have serious doubts about the methodology underlying the exercise and the results are open to more than one interpretation.

32   We accept that arrestability should be retained where offences involve Class A drugs because of the harm that these drugs do to individuals, and so that the police retain the powers necessary to obtain intelligence on suppliers and to disrupt illicit markets. The police powers related to arrestability seem essential if the major traffickers are to be brought to book. Class B drugs seem to us to present serious enough problems to justify retaining the same powers for the same reasons. With Class C drugs, however, it seems to us disproportionate and a possible violation of the European Convention of Human Rights to provide full arrestability under section 24 of PACE. It is not widely realised that it is not an offence at all to possess many of the drugs in Class C provided they are in the form of a medicinal product. Class C possession is not an arrestable offence at present and in the light of the considerations just stated we have no proposals to change this following our recommended transfer of cannabis from Class B to Class C.

33   In Scotland, since powers of arrest are not affected by our proposals, the questions are whether the effect of the present powers of detention under section 14 of the

Criminal Procedure (Scotland) Act 1995 should be retained for possession of Class B drugs; and whether they should be extended to possession of Class C drugs when cannabis is reclassified – powers of detention for possession of Class A drugs would not be affected since that would remain an imprisonable offence. We recommend, for the same reasons as we give for our recommendations on powers of arrest in England and Wales, that the effect of section 14 be preserved in Scotland for possession of Class B drugs but that it should not be extended to possession of drugs in Class C.

34   We should in any case like to see the police develop responses to illicit markets that do not involve very large numbers of stops and searches of suspected cannabis users. We doubt the efficacy of this measure at present and have received no evidence that dealers are arrested at all frequently as a result of arrests of cannabis purchasers. The present approach also seems to us to encourage such searches in contexts unrelated to illicit markets, with unwelcome consequences for relations between police and public. We accept that our proposals could increase the risk of false allegations of corruption against police officers. Although it is a risk that already exists to some extent in relation to the drugs now in Class C, moving cannabis into that Class clearly makes a great difference. But it seems to us insufficient justification for a power of arrest that it is required to protect police officers against false accusations of malpractice. We recommend that the police develop procedures for properly recording and documenting drug seizures that take place on the streets so that officers are protected against false allegations. A possible procedure, which would need further testing, would be as follows:

i)   officers seize the substance and tell suspects that they are being reported for the offence of possession;

ii)   the officer lists the substance on the stop and search slips currently being trialled by the Metropolitan Police as part of the search record and offers the suspect a copy;

iii)   the evidence is returned to the station and sealed there;

iv)   following any analysis or case disposal decision, the offender is notified by post either in the form of a summons or proposal to administer a caution.

Where the police propose to deal with the matter by way of a caution, the suspect would be invited to come to the police station for that purpose. Where the suspect refuses or fails to respond to such an invitation, the police would decide between taking no further action or submitting the papers for issue of a summons.

Premises offences

35   Under section 8 of the 1971 Act, it is an offence for the occupier or person concerned in the management of any premises knowingly to permit or suffer the following activities to take place on them:

a)   producing or attempting to produce a controlled drug;

b)   supplying or attempting to supply or offering to supply a controlled drug;

c)   preparing opium for smoking;

d)   smoking cannabis, cannabis resin or prepared opium.

The section does not attract section 28[5]. It is not, however, an absolute offence. Because it has to be committed 'knowingly', the burden is on the prosecution to prove that the accused knew that the prohibited activities were taking place. An offence against section 8 is not a drug trafficking offence for the purposes of the Drug Trafficking Act 1994. Conviction therefore does not result in confiscation under that Act, although it may lead to forfeiture under section 27 of the MDA.

36   'Premises' are not defined nor are the terms 'occupier' or 'concerned in the management' of premises. No distinction is drawn between people's homes and premises to which the public have access, for example for entertainment. Parents who allow their children to smoke cannabis are therefore liable to prosecution under section 8, as are managers of services providing treatment, care or accommodation who permit their clients to do so. The section also catches managers of dance venues who permit or suffer their customers to carry out the activities caught by section 8. The manager or occupier of premises does not have himself to be carrying out these activities. The offence essentially is that of failing to prevent others from carrying them out.

37   The range of drugs covered by each paragraph of section 8 should be noted. Paragraphs (a) and (b) apply to all controlled drugs. Paragraph (c) applies to opium only. Paragraph (d) applies only to cannabis, cannabis resin and prepared opium. The reasoning apparently was that an occupier or manager of premises may reasonably be expected to be aware of production or supply of any drugs on the premises but when drug consumption is concerned cannabis and opium are special cases because their distinctive smells make them readily detectable.

Table 5.3   Maximum penalties for premises offences

Mode of trial	Class A	Class B	Class C
(a) summary	six months or a fine of £5,000 or both	six months or a fine of £5,000 or both	three months or a fine of £2,500 or both
(b) on indictment	14 years or an unlimited fine or both	14 years or an unlimited fine or both	5 years or an unlimited fine or both

38   There are no sentencing guidelines laid down by the Court of Appeal so far as we are aware.

39   Section 8 is a means of ensuring that occupiers and people concerned in the management of premises are involved in policing the MDA. The requirement is potentially onerous. We accept, however, that production[6], supply, and dealing[7] are activities so serious that those in charge of premises may reasonably be put under an obligation not to ignore them.

---

[5]See Chapter One, paragraph 33.
[6]Subject to our views on the cultivation of cannabis, which we give in Chapter Seven, paragraphs 38-41.
[7]Under the new offence that we recommend in Chapter Four.

> ## Premises offenders: the main facts
>
> 804 persons were dealt with for premises offences in 1997, an increase of 13% over 1996 (714), and more than double the 1985 figure of 284. Cannabis was the drug involved in the overwhelming majority of cases (645 or 80% in 1997, the same proportion as in 1985). 25% of offenders were cautioned in 1997 as opposed to 10% in 1985, almost all for offences involving cannabis.
>
> Of those found guilty by the courts in 1997, 138, or 23%, were sentenced to immediate custody. This is the same as the proportion given custodial sentences in 1985; in the intervening years lower percentages were imprisoned (9% in 1990 and 17% in 1995). The average sentence in 1997 was about sixteen months, the same as in 1990, though there was a period of shorter sentences in the interval.

40   In some cases, action under the Public Entertainments Licences (Drug Misuse) Act 1997 may be the better way of proceeding. This enables a local authority to revoke a public entertainments licence with immediate effect if there is a serious problem of drug supply. But supply may take place, as may production, on premises other than places of public entertainment. If the occupiers or managers of those premises are to be made responsible for taking reasonable steps to stop them, something on the lines of section 8 (a) and (b) seems necessary. We are, however, concerned that these paragraphs may be a source of serious injustice to people who do not want drugs activities taking place on their premises but may be deemed by the courts not to have done enough to prevent them. People in charge of certain premises, particularly those used for education or the care of the homeless, sick or otherwise vulnerable, may face severe penalties for failing to prevent activities over which they have very limited control. There is also potential conflict between their duty to the people in their care and the demands of the law.

41   We recommend therefore that the section be redrafted so as to make it clear that the main aim is to deter those who wilfully allow others to supply or produce controlled drugs. The redraft should repeal the word 'suffers', which is unclear and confusing, and replace the words 'knowingly permits' with the words 'knowingly and wilfully permits' [the production or supply of controlled drugs]. 'wilfully' should be defined as meaning 'not caring whether the unlawful production or supply takes place or not'. Finally, it should be provided that a person is not to be regarded as acting wilfully merely by reason of his failure to disclose confidential records or material in respect of the persons in his care.

42   Subject to these amendments, we recommend that paragraphs (a) and (b) of section 8 be retained and extended to include the new offence of dealing that we have recommended[8]. It seems to us wrong that there should be no distinction in maximum penalties for offences involving Class A and Class B drugs and we recommend a reduction in the maximum custodial penalty on indictment for offences involving drugs in Class B from 14 years to 7.

43   Paragraphs (c) and (d) of section 8 are anomalous with the rest of the Act in that they single out use and only where opium and cannabis are concerned. The first drug is seldom used, the second is not nearly as harmful as the controlled drugs

---

[8] In Chapter Four.

that are not mentioned. This is contrary to our desired objective of a law which is consistent in its approach to the relative harms of different drugs and the activities involving them. One absurd effect of the present law is that an occupier who sees cocaine being snorted or heroin injected is committing no offence if he does nothing to prevent it while if he smells cannabis or opium he is committing an offence unless he does something to stop it.

44   One possible solution would be, as has been recommended by ACPO and others, to extend paragraphs (c) and (d) to all controlled drugs. We prefer the alternative of repealing the paragraphs altogether. This would leave the more serious activities in relation to all controlled drugs to be caught by paragraphs (a) and (b). As far as the offences of use are concerned, insofar as the law has an influence at present, it is likely to drive drug-taking out on to the streets and other places where it is potentially far less safe. Our recommendation is intended to reverse that effect.

45   Even more important, the changes that we recommend would allow active harm reduction measures and education to be provided in the entertainment venues where a very large amount of combination and stimulant drug-taking by young people occurs. The significant growth in such drug-taking in entertainment, and especially dance, venues has been one of the most notable developments in the last 25 years. These settings are of prime importance for education and harm reduction measures. We believe that it should be an obligation on the owners and managers of all premises to provide for the safety of drug-takers and that such measures should be a condition of all licences. We also think that educational material about the main drugs and their risks, including the risks of driving, should be widely available in these settings.

Opium offences

46   Section 9 of the MDA lays down opium-related offences as follows:

a)   smoking or otherwise using prepared opium;

b)   frequenting a place for the purpose of smoking opium;

c)   possession of pipes or utensils for smoking opium or preparing it for smoking.

The maximum penalties on summary conviction are 6 months imprisonment or a fine of £2,500 or both. On indictment they are they are 14 years imprisonment or a fine or both. Since the offences relate only to opium there are no Class variations. We are not aware of any sentencing guidelines laid down by the Court of Appeal.

47   Few offenders are dealt with under this section: there were none in either Scotland or Northern Ireland from 1993 to 1996 and 3 in 1997. In England and Wales 43 people were found guilty or cautioned in 1995, 11 in 1996 and 20 in 1997. 14 of those found guilty in 1997 were given sentences of immediate custody. None were cautioned.

48   In our view, section 9 should be repealed. It is anomalous in that it is the only section of the MDA which directly makes use of any drug an offence. It is also anomalous in singling out opium, presumably because of the requirements of the

Hague Convention of 1912. But opium no longer constitutes the central drugs concern that it did then, nor does the section seem necessary to satisfy the requirements of the present United Nations conventions. Opium dens, if still a problem, can be dealt with, albeit less directly, under other sections of the MDA. A further anomaly is that this section makes it an offence to *possess* (as opposed to supply as in section 9A, which we discuss below) the equipment to which it applies.

Paraphernalia

49   Section 9A, inserted into the MDA by the Drug Trafficking Offences Act 1986, is aimed at the sale of drug administration kits. It makes it an offence to supply or offer to supply any article which may be used or adapted to be used in the administration of a controlled drug, believing that the article is to be so used. There is a specific exemption for hypodermic syringes. A further offence is to supply or offer to supply articles to be used for preparing controlled drugs. 'Administration' includes administration to someone else, self-administration and self-administration with someone else's assistance. Unlike opium smoking utensils under section 9, it is not possession that is an offence but supply or an offer to supply.

50   Section 9A offences are summary only. The maximum penalty is six months imprisonment or a fine of £5,000 or both.

51   From 1993 to 1997 no person was dealt with for this offence in Scotland or Northern Ireland. In England and Wales the figures for section 9A offences in the same years never reached double figures – the highest number was 7 in 1993; in the later years the number has been 2, 3 or 4. It is not clear why prosecutions under this section are so rare. It may be that prosecution authorities see difficulty in proving that the suppliers of otherwise innocuous equipment actually believed that it would be used to administer drugs. Or the relatively low maximum penalties may have something to do with it.

52   If the offence is to be retained, we regard it as of paramount importance that the exemption for hypodermic syringes be retained and extended. This exemption is essential for the continuance of needle exchange schemes that have been so crucial in restricting the spread of HIV and other infections. The exemption should be extended so as to include other products on sale at pharmacies that can contribute to making drug use safer. A recent report by a working party set up by the Royal Pharmaceutical Society of Great Britain on pharmaceutical services for drug misusers mentions citric and ascorbic acids, water for injections, swabs, tourniquets and filters. We strongly support their recommendations.

53   There is, however, very little to be said for retaining section 9A at all. It is a dead letter. It is also inconsistent to make the sale of drug-taking equipment an offence while exempting, albeit for extremely cogent reasons, hypodermic syringes. If the exemption is widened as we and the Royal Pharmaceutical Society recommend, there will be still less purpose in keeping the section. We recommend its repeal accordingly. There might then be some scope for using section 19 (incitement) to prosecute serious cases of sale of drug administration equipment. If so, however,

we recommend that the exemption for hypodermic syringes, extended to other products as we and the Royal Pharmaceutical Society propose, should for the avoidance of doubt be inserted into section 19. There will then be no risk of pharmacists being prosecuted for inciting drug use by selling such products.

Drug-driving

54   There is emerging evidence that drug-driving is an increasingly serious problem. The Department of Environment, Transport and the Regions (DETR) published in June 1997 the preliminary results of a three-year survey designed to measure the incidence of drugs in road accident deaths. This was followed in February 1998 by the results of the first fifteen months of the survey. The preliminary results show that the monthly average number of deaths of drivers of cars and riders of two-wheel vehicles is 37 after taking illicit drugs and 27 after taking excess alcohol. This compares with figures from an equivalent survey in 1985-87 of 9 deaths on average a month after taking illicit drugs and 46 after excess alcohol.

55   The main increases have been in the number of cannabis users killed in road accidents (10% of the drivers who were killed tested positive for cannabis) and the number killed after taking two or more different types of drug. The DETR note, however, that the conclusion cannot necessarily be drawn that cannabis was a factor in all the accidents where the driver or rider tested positive for cannabis. This is because cannabis remains in the bloodstream for up to 4 weeks after it is taken by regular users, whereas its effect on driving is probably limited to at most 24 hours after it is taken. 19% of drivers who had taken illicit drugs had also taken alcohol, far less it seems than in some other countries, where 75% of drivers with cannabis in the bloodstream have been reported also testing positive for alcohol.

56   It seems to us that, because of the numbers who use it, across all social classes, cannabis driving is a special problem. As the DETR results indicate, there has been a significant increase in the number of cannabis users killed in road accidents. Unfortunately the length of time it stays in the blood make this difficult to assess with any precision, and there seem to be difficulties in developing an accurate roadside test for cannabis intoxication. The law on drug-driving is a matter primarily for road traffic legislation, not the law on drugs. Nevertheless one of our aims is to develop responsible norms of drug-driving behaviour akin to the progress that has been made in drink-driving norms among the young. The advantages of a less punitive approach to cannabis possession are that it allows for accurate health education messages and their promotion at public venues. Such messages would emphasise in particular the potential dangers of short-term cannabis intoxication, particularly if driving.

Chapter Six: Enforcement

Introduction

1 How the law is implemented is critical for its effectiveness and credibility. We have discussed penalties and sentencing, together with the offences to which they apply, in Chapters Four and Five. Penalties determine whether or not an offence is 'arrestable' under section 24 of the Police and Criminal Evidence Act 1984 (PACE). We have therefore set out in Chapter Five our recommendations on powers of arrest for possession offences alongside our recommendations for reducing the maximum penalties for those offences. In this chapter we look at two major issues in the process leading up to prosecution: police powers of stop and search – these are frequently the means by which arrests for possession are achieved; and the exercise of police discretion to caution, warn or reprimand offenders rather than prosecute. We also discuss analogous non-prosecution options in Scotland (warning letters and fiscal fines) and compounding by H.M. Customs and Excise.

Stop and search

2 Section 23 of the MDA enables a constable, if he 'has reasonable grounds to suspect that any person is in possession of a controlled drug in contravention of the Act', to 'search that person and detain him for the purpose of searching him'. The officer may also search any vehicle in which he suspects that the drug may be found and for that purpose require the person in control of the vehicle to stop it. These are discretionary powers and their impact depends on how the police exercise this discretion. Code A issued under the Police and Criminal Evidence Act 1984 (PACE) contains statutory guidelines on the exercise of this discretion and the results have been closely monitored[1]. Customs officers have separate powers to search vehicles under section 163 of CEMA and persons under section 164. They too are subject to Code A of PACE.

3 Code A gives guidance on what constitutes 'reasonable suspicion'. It says that there must be an objective basis for it. Relevant factors include time, place, behaviour and information received. People must not be judged by appearances: the code states 'reasonable suspicion can never be supported on the basis of personal factors alone without supporting intelligence or information. For example, a person's colour, age, hairstyle or manner of dress, or the fact that he is known to have a previous conviction for possession of an unlawful article, cannot be used alone or in combination with each other as the sole basis on which to search that person. Nor may it be founded on the basis of stereotyped images of certain persons or groups as more likely to be committing offences. There is an exception for members of gangs who habitually carry knives, other weapons or controlled drugs and may be recognisable by jewellery, insignias, tattoos or other features known to identify them.

---

[1]The most recent figures, with those for earlier years, are in Home Office Statistical Bulletin 2/99, *Operation of Certain Police Powers under PACE. England and Wales, 1997/8,* London, Home Office 1999.

4   In England and Wales over a million stops and searches of persons or vehicles were carried out in 1997-98 under section 1 of PACE and related legislation, including the MDA. About a third of these were for drugs. Since 1990 the numbers of stops and searches for drugs have gone up steadily, from 97,800 in 1990 to 343,900 in 1997-98. The numbers of arrests following stops and searches for drugs have also risen, from 16,000 in 1990 to 39,000 in 1997-98. But the proportion of searches leading to arrests has fallen from 16% to just under 12% in the same period. It is clear from the annual Home Office Statistics of Drug Seizures and Offenders that the great majority of such arrests followed the discovery of cannabis and the most usual outcome was a caution.

5   Of the 343,000 stops and searches for drugs in England and Wales in 1997-98, nearly half (157,230 or 46%) were carried out by the Metropolitan Police. The proportion of stops and searches leading to arrests for drugs offences varied between police forces, the lowest being 6% (Wiltshire) and the highest 27% (City of London). Most forces achieved between 11 and 14%.

6   Figures for stops and searches in Scotland[2] show that the total of persons stopped in 1998/99 was 29,045 and that drugs were found on 5,935 or 20%. This compares with a proportion of 27% on whom drugs were found in 1997/98 and 23% in 1996/97. The figures appear to be compiled on a different basis to England and Wales because there is no reference to vehicle stops.

7   Stop and search is an important means of detecting offenders. The Metropolitan Police Service examined[3] over 8000 arrest records taken from a two-month period in five London divisions. Almost 850, or just over 10%, had arisen from a stop and search. One-third of these were for drugs offences. When crimes cleared up were examined it was found that a quarter of all clear-ups for possessing drugs with intent to supply and two-thirds of those for possession had been achieved after an initial stop and search. Over 60% of all arrests following a stop and search led to a charge or caution, in 19% no further action was taken. The remaining 21% were dealt with in various other ways.

8   The question has been raised whether strip searches are permitted as part of a stop and search under section 23 of the MDA. Guidance on such searches is, however, given elsewhere in the PACE codes (Part B of Annex A to Code C, which deals with searches of people in custody at police stations). Code A has now been amended to make it clear that all searches involving exposure of intimate parts of the body shall be conducted in accordance with paragraph 11 of Annex A to Code C and not in a police van. We welcome this.

9   Home Office research[4] preceding the enactment of the Police and Criminal Evidence Act 1984 suggested that black people were three times as likely to be stopped and searched as white people. A study[5] in 1997-98 of the ten police forces in England and Wales with the highest percentage of ethnic minorities found that in these forces' areas 'overall black people were five times more likely to be stopped than whites'. In the combined Metropolitan and City of London police areas, 38 white people were stopped for every 1,000 population as compared with 66 Asian people and 181 black people.

[2]Published in the Annual Report of H.M. Chief Inspector of Constabulary for Scotland, 1998/99.
[3]*Stop and Search: Renewing the tactic. Interim Report.* Metropolitan Police Service, August 1998.
[4]C. Willis, *The use, effectiveness and impact of Police Stop and Search Powers,* Research and Planning Unit Paper no. 15. London, Home Office 1983.
[5]*Statistics on Race and the Criminal Justice System. A Home Office publication under section 95 of the Criminal Justice Act 1991,* London, Home Office 1998. Chapter Three. The results cover stops and searches for all reasons, not just drugs.

10   As the race and criminal justice system statistics[6] show, the actual number of white
people stopped and searched for any reason is still nearly eight times as large as any
other group. There are, however, significant regional variations. In inner city areas
people from the minority ethnic communities are far more likely to be stopped and
searched than elsewhere. Clearly demographic factors play some part in explaining
the far larger proportions of members of ethnic minorities searched in inner cities
as compared to the rest of England and Wales. The differential impact of stop and
search may also be as much socio-economic as racial. In our meetings with young
people we were struck by how much more often young people from the inner
London boroughs had been in contact with the police than young people in outer
London. A proportion[7] of stops and searches arise from action taken in response
to information from the public, which may be consciously or unconsciously biased.

11   We accept that the power to stop and search is essential to enforcing the law on
drugs and we have made no recommendations for any diminution of police powers
in this respect. Stop and search is a crucial evidence-gathering power. It may also
disrupt local markets and visible policing is important where trafficking is a
nuisance. But stop and search is, as the Advisory Council on the Misuse of Drugs
pointed out in 1994[8], one of the most controversial powers as well as one of the
most important.

12   The evidence to us continues to confirm the controversial nature of the power. It is
intrusive, gives opportunities for discrimination and can undermine police-
community relations. Members of the public often take exception to the manner
in which stops and searches are conducted and young people, who are particularly
prone to being stopped, see it as an unjustified interference in their freedom of
movement. It is frequently suggested that the police use their stop and search
powers as a substitute for the former 'sus' laws. The most recent research[9] suggests
that the police may sometimes use the power for intelligence gathering but that
this can seem like harassment of people who have come to police notice in the past.
The power may also be used as a form of social control for breaking up or moving
on groups of young people. None of these purposes is covered by the PACE
Codes.

13   As much resentment may be caused by the manner in which stops are made as the
fact that they take place at all. Code A has been amended to give guidance to
police officers on this point as follows:-

> '...in general a brief conversation or exchange may be desirable, not only
> as a means of avoiding unsuccessful searches, but to explain the grounds for
> the stop/search, to gain co-operation and reduce any tension there may be
> surrounding the stop/search.'

We share the view of the Advisory Council on the Misuse of Drugs[10] that the main
need is for quality control and close monitoring of the outcomes of stop and
search. The importance of monitoring and supervision is also now recognised in a
recent amendment to Code A as follows:

---

[6]See paragraph 3.10 of the report cited in the previous footnote.
[7]In the pilot sites for the study cited at footnote 9, this is put at around a quarter.
[8]*Drug Misusers and the Criminal Justice System, Part II: Police, Drug Misusers and the Community,*
London, HMSO 1994. Paragraph 3.6
[9]M. Fitzgerald, *Final Report into stop & search,* Metropolitan Police Service, 1999.
[10]See paragraph 3.10 in report cited at footnote 8.

'Supervising officers, in monitoring the exercise of officers' stop and search powers, should consider in particular whether there is any evidence that officers are exercising their discretion on the basis of stereotyped images of certain persons or groups contrary to the provisions of this Code. It is important that any such evidence should be addressed. Supervising officers should take account of the information about the ethnic origin of those stopped and searched which is collected and published under section 95 of the Criminal Justice Act 1991.'

We support the current efforts by the police to manage the tactic more fairly and effectively. The aim should be to have fewer stops and searches but a higher proportion of them with successful outcomes. Such steps are also necessary in order to ensure that powers of stop and search are compatible with the European Convention on Human Rights, since that requires powers of detention to be proportionate and objectively justifiable.

Powers of arrest

14   The powers of arrest in section 24 of the MDA now apply only in Scotland. In England and Wales they have been replaced by the powers of arrest set out in sections 24 and 25 of the Police and Criminal Evidence Act 1984 (PACE). If an offence carries a maximum penalty of imprisonment for five years or more it is an 'arrestable offence' for the purposes of section 24 of PACE. In Scotland, where PACE does not apply, police officers have powers of detention for up to six hours under section 14 of the Criminal Procedure (Scotland) Act 1995 for any offence punishable by imprisonment. This is not a power of arrest: it enables the police to detain suspects for the purpose of facilitating the carrying out of investigations. In addition section 24 of the MDA remains in force.

15   We set out these powers of arrest and detention in detail in Chapter Five because if, as we recommend, penalties for possession offences are reduced, the powers of arrest and detention that apply at present would no longer do so unless the law were amended. Even under the present law, cannabis possession offences would not be arrestable in England and Wales under section 24 of PACE or attract the power of detention in Scotland under the Criminal Procedure (Scotland) Act 1995 if, as we recommend in Chapter Three, cannabis is transferred from Class B to Class C. We have recommended that special provision outside PACE should be made to retain the present police powers of arrest in England and Wales for possession of Class A and Class B drugs. We have concluded that no change should be made to the powers of arrest for drugs in Class C. We have similarly concluded that the effect of the present powers of detention in Scotland under section 14 of the Criminal Procedure (Scotland) Act 1995 should be preserved for Class B drugs but not extended to Class C when cannabis is transferred there. Powers of arrest under our proposals will in our view remain adequate for police needs and proportionate to the offences concerned.

Use of discretion

16 The use of discretion in deciding whether or not to charge or prosecute has been of great importance in enforcement of the drugs laws in the last two decades. Had diversion, largely through cautioning, not taken place on the scale that it has done, the courts would have been unable to cope. We set out below the main features of the way discretion in this area has operated together with our conclusions on how it should be regulated in future.

Cautioning

17 The caution is the last step in a formal process. After arrest the offender is taken to the police station, where he is treated in accordance with the procedures laid down by the Police and Criminal Evidence Act 1984 and its associated codes. If, but only if, the offence is admitted, a caution may be administered (in the case of young people under the age of 18 by a uniformed Inspector in the presence of parents or an appropriate adult). In most cases the offender is released on police bail pending a decision and the caution follows at a later date.

18 A caution is not a criminal conviction but it may be cited in court as part of the defendant's criminal record. This should be explained to the offender when the caution is administered. Information about cautions may also be given in criminal *record* certificates, but not criminal *conviction* certificates, issued under Part V of the Police Act 1997. Under section 112 of this Act, the Secretary of State must issue a criminal conviction certificate to any individual who applies for one and pays a prescribed fee. The certificate gives the details of the criminal convictions of the applicant, unless they are spent under the Rehabilitation of Offenders Act 1974. Cautions should not be included since the certificate is confined to convictions. Such a certificate is likely to be needed by people whose potential employers make it a condition of employment that the applicant proves that he has no criminal record.

19 For certain appointments, the Secretary of State must issue criminal record certificates under sections 113 or 114 or enhanced criminal record certificates under sections 115 or 116 of the Police Act 1997. Examples of people who may be required to produce such certificates are those whose duties involve regular contact with children, those who need to be checked in the interests of national security, people involved in the administration of the law, people in the medical professions, people seeking appointments under the Crown and senior managers in banking and financial services. A certificate issued under section 113 may include convictions that are spent under the Rehabilitation of Offenders Act 1974 and cautions. Certificates issued under sections 114-116 may in addition contain information held on police records that does not relate to convictions or cautions at all, for example acquittals, decisions not to prosecute, continuing police operations, and known associates of the applicant.

20 There is no provision in the Rehabilitation of Offenders Act 1974 for a caution to be treated as spent. Thus a caution may remain in force after a conviction for an equivalent or more serious offence has become spent. The Government has

recently issued a consultation paper proposing that the law should be changed so that a caution becomes spent immediately, with the result that there should be no rehabilitation period for the purposes of the Act. We support this. It would mean that the recipients of a caution need not refer to it when asked, for example by a prospective employer, whether they have a criminal or police record. The caution could still, however, be cited in court during any criminal proceedings.

21   Home Office circulars giving guidance to the police on cautioning practice have encouraged consistency across police force areas and have had some success, although there are still wide variations between police forces in the proportions of offenders who are cautioned. In 1997, these varied from 22% in Dorset to 72% in Cleveland as compared with a range of 16% to 77% in 1992.

Reprimands and warnings

22   Cautions have been abolished for people under 18. Sections 65 and 66 of the Crime and Disorder Act 1998 have introduced a new system of reprimands and warnings. These apply to children under 14 and to young persons aged from 14 up to and including 17. Warnings or reprimands may be given (1) where a constable considers that on the evidence there is a reasonable prospect of conviction if the offender is prosecuted; (2) if the offender admits the offence; (3) if the offender has no previous convictions; and (4) if the constable is satisfied that it would not be in the public interest for the offender to be prosecuted.

23   A warning results in the offender being referred to a youth offending team who must assess him and, unless they consider it inappropriate, arrange for him to participate in a rehabilitation programme. Reprimands may not be given if the offender has been reprimanded or warned before. Warnings on the other hand may be repeated, but only once, provided that more than two years have passed since the previous warning. A warning may also be given in the absence of a previous reprimand if the constable thinks the offence serious enough. The provisions are being introduced in trial areas before being implemented nationally from June 2000.

24   The reprimand is similar to the caution except that repeated reprimands and reprimands of young people with previous convictions are ruled out. The warning is much more than a caution in that it requires the matter to be taken further (reference to a youth offending team and if thought appropriate a rehabilitation programme). Under subsection 66 (5) of the Act, reprimands and warnings may be cited in criminal proceedings in the same circumstances as a conviction may be cited. The position under the Rehabilitation of Offenders Act 1974 is the same as for cautions and the Government has proposed that they should be immediately spent for the purposes of the Rehabilitation of Offenders Act 1974. As with the parallel recommendation on cautions, we support this, particularly given its potential significance for the employment prospects of young people.

25   Many reprimands and warnings will be in response to offences of cannabis possession and will result in reference to youth offending teams. This is significantly different from the position with adults and for many young people it

will seem both unnecessary and disproportionate. However, early initiation into drug-taking is one of the indicators of later problem use and we recognise the advantages of a system that enables action to be taken at an early point where very young offenders are concerned.

Informal warnings etc.

26   Several police forces operate less formal warning systems. These usually involve an oral warning, sometimes without an arrest or taking the offender to the police station. An admission of guilt may be required but the offender's consent is not. Informal warnings are therefore sometimes used for offenders who refuse to accept a caution. They cannot be cited in court proceedings as part of the offender's criminal record. Many are not recorded. We were told that it was not uncommon for small quantities of cannabis found after a stop and search to be poured down the drain by the police. Presumably the motive is to save time and paperwork in what the officers concerned regard as trivial cases. As this illustrates, whatever rules are laid down it is likely that informal mechanisms will spring up to deal with cases that seem to the police not to fit those rules.

Warning letters in Scotland

27   In Scotland there is no equivalent to the formal caution nor will the provisions of the Crime and Disorder Act 1998 on reprimands and warnings apply there. Procurator fiscals may send offenders a warning letter in any case where they decide not to prosecute. There need be no admission of guilt. Warning letters may not be cited in court in criminal proceedings nor are they part of an offender's criminal record. There are no figures of the numbers issued.

Fiscal fines

28   Under section 302 of the Criminal Procedure (Scotland) Act 1995, procurator fiscals may also in lieu of prosecution offer the offender a fine (known as a 'fiscal fine') of a fixed amount for offences, including drugs offences since 1995, that are triable before a district court. There is a sliding scale, the penalties being at present £25, £50, £75 or £100. The full amount, or a predetermined instalment, is payable within 28 days. Payment is via the district court fine enforcement machinery, albeit non-payment is pursued through civil process (because no criminal conviction has taken place). Although the offender must accept the offer before any fine is enforced, no formal admission of guilt is required nor can the fiscal fine be cited in criminal proceedings. In 1997, the first year for which figures are available, 499 were accepted in drugs cases, 432 for possession of cannabis, 60 for possession of other drugs and 7 for other offences. We have been told by the Crown Office that between 60 and 70% of fiscal fines are successfully collected.

Compounding

29   Under section 152 of the Customs and Excise Management Act 1979, the Commissioners of Customs and Excise may compound proceedings for any offence under the Act (not just drugs offences). In effect this means that there will be no

prosecution provided the offender agrees to pay a monetary penalty. An admission of guilt is not required. Compounding in drugs cases is limited to offences involving herbal cannabis or cannabis resin not exceeding 10 grams in total weight. The maximum amount payable in such cases is £100.

Discretion: our conclusions

30   Drugs offences, even the most serious, cover a wide range, as our analysis in earlier chapters has shown. It is right and also in the interests of harm reduction that the least serious, which are also the ones that most frequently come to notice, should not be treated with the full rigour of the criminal law. We therefore support, on grounds both of principle and pragmatism, the approach taken by the police and customs.

31   We think, however, that discretion should operate as even-handedly as possible and that cautioning in particular needs a proper framework to achieve this. We recognise that cautioning is bound to vary considerably between different areas to reflect local diversity and local priorities. Nevertheless, we think that the differences in cautioning between police forces, although they show an improvement on several years ago, are still too wide to be equitable. Like the Royal Commission on Criminal Justice and the Advisory Council on the Misuse of Drugs[11], we recommend that cautioning should become a statutory sanction, with guidelines laid down in Regulations.

32   In the youth justice system this process is already under way with the replacement of cautions for under-18s with the new statutory system of reprimands and warnings. Even adult cautions are mentioned in statute (as in the Police Act 1997) and are likely to be included in the rehabilitation of offender provisions. What we recommend is therefore the logical conclusion to a process that has already begun.

33   Legislation would promote consistency better than non-statutory guidelines have done so far and would also, as we recommend in Chapter Eight, enable any conditions attached to a caution to be legally enforced. This is not possible at present although many police forces operate caution-plus schemes and they are recommended in the Government's 10-year drugs strategy. Legislation could also ensure that, where the offence is non-arrestable, there is power to request a person to come to the police station for the purpose of receiving a caution, although it should not be an offence to ignore such a request. We see no objection in principle to the suspect being warned that his failure to comply with a request to attend the police station for a caution to be administered might result in proceedings being instituted against him by way of summons for the offence.

Out-of-court fines

34   When a case is taken to court, a fine imposed long after the event loses much of its relevance, especially in a minor drugs case. We see attractions therefore in a procedure whereby an offender, in a case too serious to overlook or to deal with by way of caution or warning, is ordered to pay a fine of a fixed amount within 28 days. The customs and the procurator fiscal service already have this sanction at

---

[11] *Drug Misusers and the Criminal Justice System, Part II: Police, Drug Misusers and the Community,* London, HMSO 1994. Paragraph 7.33.

their disposal. We therefore recommend that, as proposed by the Royal Commission on Criminal Justice[12], the fiscal fine system be introduced in England and Wales for operation by the Crown Prosecution Service.

35   It is important that out-of-court fines should be used for cases that would otherwise be prosecuted and should not replace the caution in the kind of case for which cautions are used now. That might be ensured under the statutory cautioning guidelines that we recommend above. There would also be a question of how the fines should be paid and collected, since the CPS have no machinery for this at present. We see no objection to using the magistrates' courts machinery for this purpose provided it can respond without undue delay. We have not been told of any problems in Scotland in this respect. For the cases where it is appropriate, this innovation should be simpler, cheaper and more proportionate than prosecution.

Criminal records

36   The fiscal fine is not part of an offender's criminal record and we believe that the same should be true of all out-of-court disposals. It should be made clear in legislation that cautions, reprimands, warnings, compounds and out-of-court fines should not be capable of being cited in court as evidence of the character either of the defendant or of a witness. The principle in our view should be that only sentences passed by a court should be taken into account for that purpose. Section 66 (5) of the Crime and Disorder Act would need to be amended accordingly. A similar change is needed to CEMA's provisions on compounding in order to ensure that compounds may not as now be drawn to the attention of the court.

37   Cautions, reprimands and warnings have, however, to remain on police records if appropriate action is to be taken should the offender commit a further offence. At present, records of cautions that relate to recordable offences (roughly speaking those which carry a maximum penalty of imprisonment) are kept on the Police National Computer, while the remainder are kept on local police records. The same will apply to reprimands and warnings under the Crime and Disorder Act 1998. We think it reasonable that records of cautions, reprimands and warnings for drugs possession offences should be kept on the Police National Computer after the reduction in penalties that we propose. Otherwise, removing the maximum penalties of imprisonment for possession of Class B and Class C drugs may affect the ability of police forces to obtain access to records of previous cautions, reprimands and warnings if those took place in another police force area.

38   We make no proposals on the contents of criminal record certificates under Part V of the Police Act 1997. We note, however, that the information to be included in these is supposed to be relevant. We doubt the likely relevance in these contexts of drugs cautions, reprimands or warnings, especially if administered long in the past. We recommend therefore that the Secretary of State includes such information in the certificates only in the most exceptional cases.

---

[12]Recommendation 113.

Chapter Seven: Cannabis

Introduction

1   As the preceding chapters show, cannabis is the drug most likely to bring people into contact with the criminal justice system. It is, by far, the drug most widely and commonly used. It is the drug most often involved in the main drug offences and is the drug that is most often seized. Because of the frequent use of discretion by the police and customs, it is the drug where there is the widest gap between the law as formulated and the law as practised. Cannabis is also less harmful than the other main illicit drugs, and understood by the public to be so. If our drugs legislation is to be credible, effective and able to support a realistic programme of prevention and education, it has to strike the right balance between cannabis and other drugs.

2   Thirty years ago the Wootton Report[1] identified the crucial issue:

> 'The controversy that has arisen in the United Kingdom about the proper evaluation of cannabis in the list of psycho-active drugs, should be resolved as quickly as possible, so that both the law and its enforcement as well as programmes of health education, may be relevant to what is known about the dangers of cannabis-smoking in this country, and may receive full public support.'

This is the task that we set ourselves in this chapter. In it we bring together the evidence which appears at many different points in this report, and which forms the basis of our conclusions. In this chapter, except in the section on therapeutic uses, we discuss cannabis only in its natural plant form, that is herbal cannabis and cannabis resin.

Prevalence, availability and price

3   Three successive British Crime Surveys (in 1994, 1996 and 1998) show that cannabis is, by far, the drug most likely to have been used by all age groups in the last month, last year or at any time. A 1998 survey of 11 to 15 year-old[2] school children suggests that taking cannabis is relatively rare among 11-13 year-olds, but increases from the age of 14.

4   Younger people aged 16 to 29 are more likely than those aged 30 and older to say that they have used drugs. About one in five people aged 16-29 in England and Wales say they have used cannabis in the last year, and one in eight say they have used it in the last month (British Crime Surveys since 1994). An estimated two and a half million 16-29 year olds used cannabis at least once last year, and around a million and a half used it least once last month (based on the 1998 British Crime Survey).

5   In their evidence to the House of Lords Select Committee on Science and Technology[3], the Department of Health said 'cannabis is now the third most

---

[1] *Cannabis. Report by the Advisory Committee on Drug Dependence,* London, HMSO 1968, paragraph 68.
[2] Office of National Statistics, *Smoking, Drinking and Drugs Use Among Young Teenagers,* London, The Stationery Office 1999.
[3] *Cannabis. The Scientific and Medical Evidence,* London, The Stationery Office 1998. (HL Paper 151, November). Paragraph 6.3.

commonly consumed drug after alcohol and tobacco'. The House of Lords report noted that the extent of cannabis use in the United Kingdom is not dissimilar to that in other European countries and somewhat lower than in the United States, Canada and Australia.

6 Both our MORI surveys and our meetings with young people make it clear that there is no difficulty in obtaining the drug, nor is there any sense that the law is a deterrent for the majority. This is so despite record levels of seizures by police and customs. In 1997, 77% of all drugs seized were cannabis – 150,000 kg. were seized by customs and the police as well as 115,000 plants, almost all seized by the police. In 1990 the comparable figures were 31,000 kg. of cannabis and 34,000 plants.

7 Despite these efforts, the average price of cannabis appears to have been virtually unaffected, decreasing slightly according to the National Criminal Intelligence Service between December 1997 and December 1998, although there are significant local and regional variations. Whether in herbal or resin form, cannabis is commonly sold to consumers in fractions of an ounce, with a deal consisting of 1/8 of an ounce. The evidence suggests that 60% of sales are in the form of resin, 40% in the form of herbal cannabis (of which 60-70% is said to be home grown). The present average price of a 1/8 ounce is put at between £5 and £25 depending upon the form of the substance and its purported potency.

8 We have considered the evidence put to the House of Lords Select Committee on Science and Technology[4] on the potency of cannabis in its various natural plant forms. The evidence is conflicting. It appears that, while some forms of herbal cannabis grown by hydroponic methods may have concentrations of tetrahydrocannabinol (THC), the main psychoactive ingredient of cannabis, of as much as 20%, the average THC content in both herbal cannabis and cannabis resin as analysed by the Forensic Science Service from seizures by the police is around 4-5%. There is no evidence that the presence of THC in higher concentrations leads to significantly higher health risks, just as it cannot be claimed that the risks would be eliminated if only lower-strength varieties of cannabis were available.

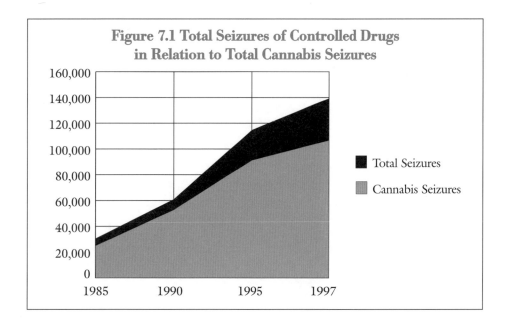

Figure 7.1 Total Seizures of Controlled Drugs in Relation to Total Cannabis Seizures

[4]Report cited in footnote 3, paragraphs 6.11-6.15.

Relative harmfulness of cannabis

9   The main issue for any consideration of the current law on cannabis is how harmful
     it is compared with other major illicit drugs and whether that harm is properly
     reflected in the law. We have consulted a wide range of addiction specialists on the
     relative harm of the major drugs. We asked them to compare drugs independently
     of their legal classification. The specialists' views underpin the legal classification of
     cannabis that we propose[5]. We have also carefully considered the work of other
     experts, including the written and oral evidence presented to the House of Lords.
     We regard the following conclusions as a fair representation of the current weight
     of professional opinion.

10   Cannabis is not a harmless drug. That is not in dispute. We cannot do better than
     quote the summary of harms from cannabis set out by the House of Lords:

> '...cannabis is neither poisonous..., nor highly addictive, and we do not
> believe that it can cause schizophrenia in a previously well user with no
> predisposition to develop the disease. However, we are satisfied that:
>
> - It is intoxicating enough to impair the ability to carry out safety-critical
>   tasks (such as flying, driving or operating machinery) for several hours
>   after taking...;
>
> - It can have adverse psychic effects ranging from temporary distress,
>   through transient psychosis, to the exacerbation of pre-existing mental
>   illness...;
>
> - Regular use can lead to psychological dependence...; and, in some
>   dependent individuals (perhaps 5-10 per cent of regular users), regular
>   heavy use can produce a state of near continuous intoxication, making
>   normal life impossible;
>
> - Withdrawal may occasionally involve unpleasant symptoms...;
>
> - Cannabis impairs cognitive function during use...;
>
> - It increases the heart rate and lowers the blood pressure, carrying risks
>   to people with cardiovascular conditions, especially first-time users who
>   have not developed tolerance to this effect....
>
> ...In addition, smoking cannabis carries similar risks of respiratory disorders
> to smoking tobacco.[6]'

11   There is considerable concern that cannabis use may contribute to transport
     accidents since laboratory tests show it can impair performance including driving.
     However, a review of the scientific literature on drugs and driving commissioned
     by the European Monitoring Centre for Drugs and Drug Addiction (EMCDDA)[7]
     found that evidence as to whether cannabis impairs driving and increases the risk of
     road accidents was not entirely consistent. Some studies found no significant
     effects on perception, and others pointed to some impairment of attention and
     short-term memory, although these effects are typically observed at higher doses.
     Still others suggest that drivers under the influence of cannabis actually drive more
     carefully. Interpretation of the causal contribution of cannabis to road accidents is
     further complicated by the concurrent presence of other drugs, especially alcohol.

---

[5]See Chapter Three, paragraph 31.
[6]See paragraphs 8.19 and 8.21 of the report cited at footnote 3.
[7]*Annual Report on the State of the Drugs Problem in the European Union 1999*. Luxembourg, Office of
Official Publications of the European Union, 1999. Page 28.

12   This situation may change if use increases and the most recent Department of
      Environment Transport and the Regions report on road traffic deaths shows more
      cannabis positive cases as compared with ten years ago. Moreover, ongoing
      research suggests that when cannabis and alcohol are taken together, their effects
      on driving are at least additive, and that they may even increase each other's
      effects. We therefore support the active discouragement of driving under the
      influence of cannabis, especially when in combination with alcohol.

Long-term risks

13   There are also long-term risks. It is worth noting the increasing numbers
      presenting themselves for treatment for problems brought on by cannabis use. The
      regional drug misuse databases[8] show that the number of people seeking help from
      a wide range of drug agencies for problems with cannabis use has doubled from
      1,400 in 1993 (7% of the total seeking help) to 3,300 in 1998, (10% of the total).
      This is, of course, a small fraction of the total number of people who take cannabis
      but the results must not be discounted. The figures show people who identified
      cannabis as their 'main drug' when seeking help. They do not, however, reveal the
      nature of the problems for which the help was sought.

The gateway theory

14   Perhaps the most serious charge against cannabis is made by the so-called 'gateway
      theory'. This argues that cannabis use leads to the use of more dangerous drugs
      such as heroin and cocaine. The basic idea of the gateway theory comes from the
      observation that most users of heroin and other hard drugs have a history of using
      cannabis. In addition, various mechanisms have been suggested to explain the
      supposed tendency of users to move from cannabis to harder drugs. One such
      mechanism is said to lie in the structure of illegal markets, which leads dealers to
      encourage cannabis users to try other drugs in the hope of increasing profits.
      Another suggestion is that the pharmacological action of cannabis somehow
      predisposes the users to try other drugs. We examine these suggestions below.

15   It is certainly true that the use of hallucinogens, amphetamines, cocaine and heroin
      is almost always preceded by experimentation with cannabis use. It also seems that
      the earlier the initiation into cannabis, and the greater the involvement with it, the
      greater the likelihood of progression to the use of other drugs. But these facts are
      not nearly enough to support the gateway theory. The theory has to show that
      there is a high probability that a cannabis user will become a heroin user, not just
      that there is a high probability that a heroin user has been a cannabis user. In fact,
      the vast majority of cannabis users do not progress to the most dangerous drugs
      such as heroin. Any significant causal relationship in that direction would have
      resulted in a far higher population of hard drug users than we have.

16   In our view nothing has emerged to disturb the conclusions of the Advisory
      Committee on Drug Dependence in 1968[9], when they said that there was no
      convincing evidence that cannabis use in itself led to heroin use. This has been
      largely confirmed by more recent studies. The World Health Organisation noted
      in 1997[10] that in some countries there had been a predictable sequence of

---

[8]See Chapter Two, paragraphs 14 and 15 for a fuller account.
[9]Paragraph 6.3 of the report cited at footnote 1.
[10]*Cannabis: a health perspective and research agenda*. Geneva, World Health Organisation, 1997. Section 5.4.

adolescent drug use with cannabis preceding the use of other drugs including cocaine and heroin but that this

> 'does not imply that a high proportion of those who experiment with cannabis will go on to use heroin, for example'.

Studies have also shown that cannabis is seldom the first drug that people take for recreational purposes. They almost invariably start with cigarettes or alcohol or both[11]. There is good evidence that the likelihood of 11 to 15 year-olds having ever used an illicit drug is strongly related to regular underage smoking and drinking[12].

17   The suggestion, already mentioned, that there are pharmacological properties of cannabis that predispose users of it to later heroin use, has been discounted in a recent review of the United States literature[13]. Taking cannabis is not by itself an indicator of future heroin or cocaine use unless the cannabis use is heavy and combined with psychiatric or conduct disorders and a family history of psychopathology.

18   Social, cultural and market conditions associated with cannabis use are a different matter. It may be that some cannabis users will go on to other drugs through the influence of friends or the pressure of other factors associated with problematic drug use, such as poverty and unemployment. The WHO concluded that the most plausible explanation for some cannabis users also using other drugs was

> '....a combination of selective recruitment into cannabis use of non-conforming and deviant adolescents who have a propensity to use illicit drugs, and the socialisation of cannabis users within an illicit drug-using subculture which increases the opportunity and encouragement to use other illicit drugs.'

In particular, we take seriously the suggestion that pressure may be exercised by dealers on cannabis users to try harder drugs. If there is anything at all in the gateway theory, it is likely to be found in the structure of illegal markets.

19   There is no evidence that cannabis use is crime-related in the same way as heroin or crack cocaine. Nevertheless, when people are arrested for other crimes, cannabis is frequently found in their possession or traces of it detected in their urine through analysis. In a study of a sample of 622 offenders arrested in five police areas in 1996/97[15], cannabis was the most common illicit drug found in their urine. 46% of those arrested tested positive for it compared with between 72% and 82%, depending on the area, testing positive for alcohol. No particular offence was typical of those testing positive for cannabis and they were not heavily involved with acquisitive crime. Given the wide prevalence of cannabis use in the population at large (and even more so among the age groups likeliest to be committing crime) this is hardly surprising. The difficulty of assessing the significance of drugs in drug-related crime lies in the absence of any evidence that it is the drug that causes the crime rather than other factors also associated with criminality.

---

[11]D.B. Kandel and others "Stages of progression of drug involvement from adolescence to adulthood: further evidence for the gateway theory", *Journal of Studies on Alcohol,* (53) 1992, pp.447-457.
[12]See report cited at footnote 2.
[13]Institute of Medicine, *Marijuana and medicine: assessing the science base.* Washington, D.C., National Academy Press 1999. Chapter Three.
[14]See paragraph 5.4 of report cited in footnote 10.
[15]T. Bennet, *Drugs and crime: the results of research on drug testing and inverviewing arrestees,* Home Office Research Study 183, London, Home Office 1998.

Overall assessment of the harmfulness of cannabis

20   The British Medical Association has said[16] 'The acute toxicity of cannabinoids is extremely low: they are very safe drugs and no deaths have been directly attributed to their recreational or therapeutic use.' The Lancet published an article[17] summarising the evidence on the most probable adverse health and psychological consequences of acute and chronic use, and its editorial in the same issue comments that '...on the evidence summarised by Hall and Solowij, it would be reasonable to judge cannabis less of a threat than alcohol or tobacco....We...say that, on the medical evidence available, moderate indulgence in cannabis has little ill-effect on health, and that decisions to ban or legalise cannabis should be based on other considerations.'

21   New medical and scientific knowledge can still be expected to add to the evidence of long-term harm from cannabis, despite the length of time it has been available and the extent of its use. Nevertheless, as the House of Lords report remarks, the harms must not be overstated. When cannabis is systematically compared with other drugs against the main criteria of harm (mortality, morbidity, toxicity, addictiveness and relationship with crime), it is less harmful to the individual and society than any of the other major illicit drugs or than alcohol and tobacco. This is why our consideration of the relative harmfulness of drugs has led us to the conclusion that cannabis is wrongly placed in Class B of Schedule 2 to the MDA.

22   These conclusions are also consistent with public perceptions of the comparative harm of individual drugs. As the surveys conducted for us by MORI show[18], children below the age of 15 see cannabis as almost as harmful as other drugs. From the age of about 15 or 16, however, though their perceptions of other drugs remain stable, their views on cannabis change remarkably. About 34% of 16 to 59 year-olds in our older sample considered cannabis harmful or very harmful, far fewer than those who held that view about other illicit drugs (90-98% depending on the drug) and about alcohol (67%) and tobacco (84%).

The Law on Cannabis

The United Nations Conventions

23   We have set out[19] the general implications of the United Nations conventions and discussed them further[20] in relation to trafficking and possession offences. For cannabis the implications may be summed up as follows:

i)   cannabis, cannabis resin and extracts and tinctures of cannabis are included in Schedule I to the Single Convention while cannabis and cannabis resin are also included in Schedule IV. The main MDA offences have therefore to apply to cannabis as to other drugs;

ii)   but there is no requirement to place cannabis in one Class rather than another in the MDA, not least because the imposition of penalties is largely a matter of domestic law. It is already dissociated from the other Single Convention Schedule I drugs, most of which are Class A;

[16] *Therapeutic uses of cannabis,* Amsterdam, Harwood Academic Publishers 1997. Page 65.
[17] W. Hall and N. Solowij, 'Adverse effects of cannabis', *The Lancet* 14 November 1998, pp. 1611-1616.
[18] See Chapter Two, paragraphs 59-61.
[19] See Chapter One, paragraphs 5-14.
[20] See Chapter Four, paragraphs 6 and 7, and Chapter Five, paragraphs 2 to 6.

iii) imprisonment is not required by the conventions as a sanction either for possession or for cultivation for personal consumption. Alternatives to conviction and punishment may be considered, including treatment, education, aftercare, rehabilitation, or social reintegration;

iv) some trafficking offences where cannabis is involved may also be 'appropriate cases of a minor nature' where the same alternatives to conviction and punishment could be considered;

v) for reasons that we explain in detail below, it would be possible without renegotiating the conventions to permit the therapeutic use of cannabis, cannabis resin or extracts and tincture of cannabis. The conventions do, however, prevent the prescription of cannabinols (except nabilone and dronabinol) for medical treatment.

The UK law on cannabis

24 Under the MDA, cannabis and cannabis resin are placed in Class B. Those in possession can incur a maximum prison term on indictment of 5 years with an unlimited fine. Traffickers may incur 14 years and an unlimited fine with a liability to confiscation of assets in addition. Growers may also be sentenced to 14 years and treated as traffickers because they are normally prosecuted for production under section 4 of the MDA, not for cultivation under section 6. The owners or managers of premises who knowingly permit or suffer the smoking of cannabis are also exposed to a maximum prison term on indictment of 14 years.

25 If, as we argue, the present classification of cannabis is not justified, it follows that the response of the law is disproportionate to the drug's harm, and may bring the law into disrepute.   In our view, therefore, the maximum penalties for cannabis offences should be reduced. This would bring them more into line with penalties in other European countries.

The operation of the law on cannabis

26 The number of people dealt with for drugs offences involving cannabis rose from 40,194 in 1990 to 86,034 in 1997.   This was an increase of 114% and represented 76% of all drugs offences in 1997.

27 Enforcing the drugs laws, especially against the possession of cannabis, inevitably involves the police in large numbers of stop and searches.   Over 300,000 were carried out for drugs in 1996-97 in England and Wales, bringing the total for four years to over a million. These resulted, over that period, in 134,500 arrests where drugs were found – the great majority of which were for cannabis. While the number of stop and searches has grown, the proportion where drugs have been found and arrests made has declined from 18% in 1988 to 12% in 1997/8[21]. Stops and searches bear disproportionately on young people from minority ethnic communities in inner city areas. They certainly appear to be discriminatory, although there may be demographic and socio-economic reasons which would make it hard to eliminate the appearance of discrimination altogether.

[21]Home office Statistical Bulletin 2/99, *Operation of Certain Police Powers under PACE: England and Wales 1997/8.* London, Home Office 1999.

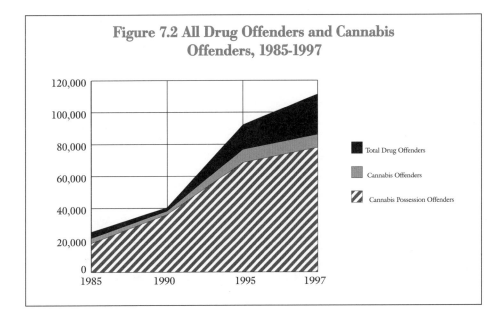

Figure 7.2 All Drug Offenders and Cannabis Offenders, 1985-1997

Diversion from prosecution

28 Many cases are kept away from the courts by cautioning and compounding and, in Scotland, warning letters and fiscal fines. By far the largest increase in police cautioning in England and Wales has been for cannabis offenders, from 41% in 1990 to 55% in 1997. This has meant in practice a tripling in the number of cannabis offenders for which a caution was given, from 16,500 to 47,000. Cautions are part of an offender's criminal record. There is no provision at present for these records to expire under the Rehabilitation of Offenders Act 1974. The Government has recently issued a consultation paper proposing that this anomaly should be corrected and that cautions should be immediately spent. This would also apply to reprimands and warnings, which are to replace cautions for young people under 18 under the Crime and Disorder Act 1998.

29 Cautioning is not used by H.M. Customs and Excise or in Scotland. For importation and exportation offences, compounding – a monetary penalty in lieu of prosecution – may be used in cases involving cannabis not exceeding 10 grams in weight. While compounding does not necessarily become part of an offender's criminal record, it may be mentioned in subsequent court proceedings. Its use for cannabis importation offenders fell between 1990 and 1997 from 58% to 45%.

30 In Scotland, the procurator fiscal service which brings prosecutions in criminal cases may, if the offender agrees, offer a fine instead of prosecution. Such fines have only recently been used in drugs cases and in 1997, the first year for which figures are available, fines were accepted by 432 of 499 persons dealt with for possession of cannabis.

31 This discretion in the implementation of the MDA is desirable but produces anomalies in the differing regimes of cautioning and compounding, and inconsistencies in the cautioning rates between police forces. More than half of the arrests for cannabis offences result in a caution. We do not criticise the police for their extensive use of cautioning. It is currently the only realistic and proportional

response. Without it, the courts would have ground to a halt. However, the use of discretion does not lessen the disproportionate attention that the law and the implementation of the law unavoidably give to cannabis and cannabis possession in particular.

32   Even with the use of discretion on this scale, the law's implementation damages individuals in terms of criminal records and risks to jobs and relationships to a degree that far outweighs any harm that cannabis may be doing to society. Moreover young people, particularly young black and Asian people and particularly where stop and search is concerned, perceive the law as unfair.

33   Discretion needs a clear framework in which to operate. That is why we recommend that cautioning be put on a statutory footing, with guidelines in regulations. This has already been done for people under 18 in the provisions of the Crime and Disorder Act 1998. We do not favour less use of discretion. Better the present, somewhat informal, arrangements than a tightening up that leads to more people being brought needlessly into the criminal justice system.

Sentencing of offenders

34   Even with diversions from prosecution on the present scale, between 1990 and 1997 large numbers of cases involving cannabis, 38,000 in 1997 – far more than any other drug - continued to be tried by the courts. Between 1990 and 1997, the proportion of people fined after being found guilty of cannabis offences fell from 67% to 49%. The proportion imprisoned rose from 10% to 14%. Despite Court of Appeal guidelines recommending fines as the normal penalty for cannabis possession, fines for possession – by far the most frequent offence – declined markedly from 70% to 55% of cases. Over the period there was a small rise in the proportion sentenced to imprisonment, from 6% to 8%. While the reasons for imprisonment are not completely clear, there are indications that almost no one is given an immediate custodial sentence solely for possession of cannabis, unless there is evidence of persistent flouting of the law.

35   Between 1990 and 1997, the likelihood of being imprisoned for the more serious, mainly trafficking, offences increased and the likelihood of being fined declined. For example, the proportion of people fined for production of cannabis fell from 63% to 37%, while the percentage given immediate custodial sentences rose from 6% to 16%. The proportion of offenders fined for allowing premises to be used for cannabis offences halved to 22% in 1997, while the percentage given sentences of immediate custody more than doubled to 19%.

36   The concentration on cannabis as an objective of law enforcement is at odds with the views of a significant proportion of the population. The surveys conducted for us by MORI show that two-thirds of adults want strong legal controls on drugs and do not regard drug use as a private matter beyond the law. But most of them do not include cannabis among the drugs that need controlling. Almost one-half (46%) thought that the law should be changed so that it is not against the law to use it. When asked to select three things they thought should be the highest priorities for the police, less than 1% of respondents mentioned cannabis use as

opposed to 8% who selected heroin use. Only 9% chose cannabis dealing as compared to 66% who chose heroin dealing. 54% said that cannabis use should be the lowest priority as compared to 1% who said that heroin use should be.

37   In considering the current operation of the law and sentencing patterns we are of the view that the possession of cannabis should not be an imprisonable offence. Consequentially, it should no longer be an arrestable offence in England and Wales under section 24 of PACE. Further, the prosecution of offences of cannabis possession should be the exception and only then should an offence, if there is a conviction, incur a criminal record.

Cultivation of cannabis

38   Cultivation of cannabis is a separate offence under section 6 of the MDA but cases are generally prosecuted under section 4 (2) as production. This was not the position in 1971. The definition of cannabis covered only the flowering or fruiting tops of the plant, with the result that a person found growing plants that had not yet flowered or produced fruiting tops was not guilty of production, though he could be prosecuted for cultivation. Section 52 of the Criminal Law Act 1977 widened the definition of cannabis in the MDA to include almost the whole plant. Since then, cases have been brought under section 4; section 6 has become virtually a dead letter.

39   This change is more than a legal technicality because production, but not cultivation of cannabis, is designated as a trafficking offence for the purposes of the Drug Trafficking Act 1994. Confiscation of assets may result from a conviction. This may be disproportionate in cases involving a few plants for personal use. Although we have heard no reports of the courts ordering confiscation in such cases, the law as it stands seems to allow the possibility.

40   This situation is not required by the United Nations conventions. The 1988 convention against illicit traffic in narcotic drugs and psychotropic substances[22] permits two separate offences: one of cultivation for the purpose of the production of narcotic drugs (in effect the trafficking offence); the other cultivation for personal consumption (an offence for which imprisonment as a sanction is not required). This approach to cannabis cultivation seems clear and logical compared with that of the MDA. There are real differences, which United Kingdom law does not currently reflect, between activities that are production for the purposes of supply, and those that are cultivation for personal use.

41   We recommend that the cultivation of small numbers of cannabis plants for personal use should be a separate offence from production, and should be treated in the same way as possession of cannabis.

International Comparisons

42   In coming to our conclusions we were influenced by the experience of other countries. The position in the Netherlands has been of particular interest as the country where tolerance of cannabis has been taken furthest. Dutch law divides drugs into two classes. One class includes all the drugs defined as carrying an

---

[22]See Chapter One, paragraph 9 and 10.

unacceptable risk. The other class contains all the other drugs. The maximum penalties for offences involving the possession of drugs in this second class are significantly milder, one month's detention as opposed to one year. The main aim of the law is to ensure that drug users are not caused more harm by prosecution and imprisonment than by the use of the drugs themselves.

43 Dutch drugs policy is aimed at separating the market for less harmful drugs – herbal cannabis and cannabis resin – from the market for drugs carrying an unacceptable risk – such as heroin and cocaine. The Dutch reject the idea that cannabis pharmacologically induces people to switch from soft to hard drugs. They do, however, accept that the more that users are part of a subculture where drugs of both classes are obtainable, the greater the risk of progression from soft to hard drugs.

44 Within this framework, the sale of cannabis from licensed or regulated coffee shops, for use either on or off the premises, is tolerated. The coffee shops and their regulation are seen as consistent with a broader public information and education policy. This is based on accurate information about the risks of drug use, as well as of alcohol and tobacco, and ways of limiting those risks.

45 There is a 5 gram limit on individual sales (originally 30 grams but reduced in 1995), and a 500 gram limit on the coffee shop stocks. Although possession and supply remain offences, prosecution is waived in the public interest provided these amounts are not exceeded under a formal written policy based on the principle of expediency. Other conditions that have to be met if the coffee shop is to remain in business are:

i)   no sales of hard drugs;

ii) no sales to minors;

iii) no advertising;

iv) no sales of alcohol on the same premises;

v)   no nuisance (specific local rules may be set about such matters as parking in front of the entrance or early closing times).

46 If coffee shops violate these conditions they risk being closed down, and since 1996 the number of coffee shops has been reduced by between 10% and 15%. There is a tripartite approach involving the local authority, police, and public prosecutor to deal with issues arising from the regulation of coffee shops.

47 Holland's formal written policy of not prosecuting people found in possession of small amounts of cannabis dates from 1976, with coffee shop sales tolerated from 1980. It was not followed immediately by increases in the numbers using the drug. But, beginning in 1984, use increased sharply following increasing commercialisation. Increases in use in Holland since the early 1990s have paralleled increases taking place in the United States and in other countries with stricter enforcement policies. The recent publication of the survey of drug-taking prevalence in Holland[23] shows that the number of people ever taking cannabis there, or taking it in the last month, is significantly lower than that shown in the 1998 British Crime Survey.

---

[23] *Licit and illicit drug use in the Netherlands, 1997.* Centrum voor Drugsonderzoek, Universiteit van Amsterdam. 1999.

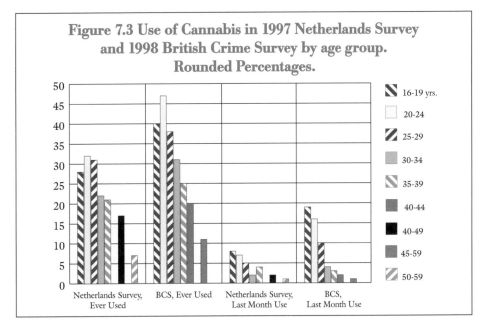

Figure 7.3 Use of Cannabis in 1997 Netherlands Survey and 1998 British Crime Survey by age group. Rounded Percentages.

Legend:
- 16-19 yrs.
- 20-24
- 25-29
- 30-34
- 35-39
- 40-44
- 40-49
- 45-59
- 50-59

48 The following results are claimed for the Dutch drug policy:

i) Although cannabis use has increased since the coffee shop policy was introduced, similar or greater increases have taken place in other countries including the United Kingdom, the United States, the former West Germany, France, Spain, Sweden and Finland[24];

ii) self-reported cannabis use amongst the youngest surveyed age group (16-19 years) is consistently lower in the Netherlands than the United Kingdom;

iii) the number of problem drug users has been stable for many years, and the average age of this group in Amsterdam has risen year on year and is now 36. (United Kingdom data suggest annually increasing numbers of problem drug users, the average age of new addicts is 25 or 26, while between 1991 and 1996 the proportion under 21 rose from 15% to 22%);

iv) drug-related deaths per million population are the lowest in Europe. In 1995, the figure for the Netherlands was 2.4 as against 31.1 for the United Kingdom. (We recognise the difficulty of comparing mortality statistics between countries on a like for like basis but the relative success of the Netherlands seems undeniable on any conceivable interpretation).

49 The coffee shop approach has not been without critics even in Holland itself. It seems, however, that Holland can justly claim to have separated the heroin and cannabis markets. As a result, young people are far less likely in Holland than elsewhere to experiment with heroin. Although there is room for argument over how precisely this has been achieved, it is difficult to deny that the policy of separation of markets, including the toleration of coffee shops, has made a contribution.

50 It should be noted that it is not certain that most sales of cannabis take place through the coffee shop system – one estimate puts the proportion at a third. We cannot therefore be certain that it is the policy of market separation that has achieved the Dutch success with heroin, although the possibility is a very real one.

---

[24]The best data for this comparison are to be found in the Annual Reports of the European Monitoring Centre for Drugs and Drugs Addiction. Care must be taken in interpreting the data as there are differences between countries in the survey years, drugs covered and age range of samples.

The same success in separating cannabis from heroin is not claimed for other drugs, particularly cocaine, amphetamines and ecstasy.

51   The coffee shop mechanism is difficult to reconcile fully with the requirements of the United Nations conventions. The policy of non-prosecution for the sale and possession of small amounts can be justified on the basis that the prosecution of offences is left to domestic law, under which discretion may be exercised if it is expedient in the public interest. A similar public interest criterion is applied by United Kingdom prosecutors. It is less easy to justify the holding of stocks of cannabis by coffee shops, and their supply through cultivation or importation (about half from each). The supply, at least, seems to take place in breach of the law.

52   Despite these difficulties and contradictions, we think that the Dutch experience holds two important lessons for the United Kingdom. The first is the potential benefit from treating the possession and personal use of all drugs – not just cannabis – primarily as health problems. This should ensure that young people who experiment with drugs remain integrated into society rather than becoming marginalised. The second is the potential benefit from separating the market for cannabis from that of heroin. By doing so, the Dutch have provided persuasive evidence against the gateway theory of cannabis use, and in favour of the theory that if there is a gateway it is the illegal market place.

53   We recognise that, in the present political and cultural climate, it is difficult to see the introduction of Dutch-style coffee shops in the United Kingdom. The contradictions between domestic and international law and these practices are too great. The Dutch may be able to live with them, but they are likely to cause greater difficulties here. Nevertheless there may be developments that move us towards the Dutch experience, particularly as greater autonomy is devolved to local communities.

54   Other international comparisons suggest that the law has a limited effect, if any, on use[25]. During the 1970s several states in the U.S.A. reduced the maximum penalty for the first offence of possession of small amounts of marijuana for personal use to a small fine. Levels of marijuana use increased between 1972 and 1977 in those states but even more so in the states that had not reduced penalties. In fact the greatest rises in use took place in states with the most severe penalties.

55   Since 1987, South Australia has operated a cannabis expiation notice (CEN) scheme under which the payment of a small fine within 60 days enables offenders over 18 to avoid prosecution. The expiable offences include offences consistent with personal use. The number of notices issued under the scheme doubled between 1987 and 1996, probably due to the greater ease of CEN procedures compared with the arrest and charge procedures required for prosecution. In response to a decline in the rate at which fines were paid between 1987 and 1991/2 new legislation was introduced in 1996 intended to increase the rate of expiation by allowing the offender a greater range of payment options. Figures to 1995 indicated that there was an increase in cannabis use since the beginning of the CEN scheme. However, there were also increases over the same period in two

[25]E.Single. 'The impact of marijuana decriminalisation: an update'. *Journal of Health Policy*, (Winter, 1989), pages 456-466.

other states where penalties had not changed.   There were no greater increases either in weekly cannabis use or in use among 14 to 29 year olds in South Australia compared with the rest of the country[26].

Therapeutic use of cannabis

56   Until 1973, tincture of cannabis had been available for medical use for over 100 years. In 1973, the medical use of cannabis was prohibited in the United Kingdom following a long decline in its use in favour of what were considered more reliable drugs. Beginning in the 1980s, interest in the potential benefits of cannabis for the treatment of certain medical conditions was renewed, and has become a significant issue. The medical and scientific basis for this increased interest has been considered by the British Medical Association[27] and the House of Lords[28]. We have nothing to add to the detail of the reports of the expert members of both of these bodies. However, we recognise the importance of careful consideration of the issue because of the implications that therapeutic use of cannabis has for the MDA.

57   Cannabis, cannabis resin, cannabinol, and cannabinol derivatives are listed in Schedule 1 to the Misuse of Drugs Regulations 1985 (except dronabinol or its stereoisomers which are now in Schedule 2 of the regulations). In effect, this means that these substances cannot lawfully be produced, supplied, possessed, imported or prescribed except under licence from the Secretary of State issued under Regulation 5. The drugs are also designated by order under section 7 (4) of the MDA as drugs whose production, supply and possession are unlawful for any purpose other than research.

58   Two cannabinoid-type substances can be prescribed by doctors as part of the treatment of their patients. The first is nabilone. This is not a controlled drug. It is a synthetic analogue of THC which is licensed under the Medicines Act 1968 for prescription to patients with nausea or vomiting resulting from cancer chemotherapy and which has proved unresponsive to other drugs. The second is dronabinol, which is a synthetic THC in sesame oil and appears in Schedule 2 to the 1985 regulations. This allows it to be prescribed on a named-patient basis for the same purpose as nabilone.

59   The United Nations conventions are restrictive but there is more room for manoeuvre in the case of cannabis and cannabis resin than there is over cannabinols. Cannabis and cannabis resin are contained in Schedule IV to the Single Convention. Article 2.5 (b) of this states 'A Party shall, if in its opinion the prevailing conditions in its country render it the most appropriate means of protecting the public health and welfare, prohibit the production, manufacture, export and import, trade in, possession or use of any [Schedule IV] drug except for amounts which may be necessary for medical and scientific research only, including clinical trials therewith to be conducted under or subject to the control of the Party.' This does not impose a mandatory obligation on the United Kingdom to prohibit any of those activities in relation to cannabis or cannabis resin because it is subject to the proviso that the prevailing conditions in the country concerned make it the most appropriate means of protecting the public health and welfare.

---

[26]R. Ali, et al., *The social impacts of the Cannabis Expiation Notice scheme in South Australia.*
Canberra: Department of Health and Family Services 1998.
[27]See report cited at footnote 16.
[28]See report cited at footnote 3.

For example, heroin, another drug contained in schedule IV to the Single Convention, is in fact available on prescription in the United Kingdom for the treatment of organic disease or injury.

60   The position with cannabinoids is different. They are listed in schedule I of the 1972 United Nations Convention on Psychotropic Substances. Article 7 (a) of this requires states to 'prohibit all use except for scientific and very limited medical purposes by duly authorised persons, in medical or scientific establishments which are directly under the control of their Governments or specifically approved by them'. There is no saving for 'prevailing conditions' in the country concerned and the requirement is therefore binding. Because of it dronabinol had to be moved from Schedule I of the 1972 convention, before it was possible for the United Kingdom government, in 1995, to put it in Schedule 2 to the 1985 Regulations, thus allowing its prescription for medical purposes.

61   To summarise, the government has the power to allow cannabis and cannabis resin, including tinctures and extracts, to be prescribed in this country without renegotiation of the international conventions. But for cannabinols other than dronabinol and nabilone to be used therapeutically, the conventions would have to be renegotiated first.

62   The British Medical Association concluded[29] that cannabis in its plant form was unsuitable for medical use. The grounds were

a)   cannabis contains over 400 chemical compounds and over 60 cannabinoids. Even if proved to have therapeutic benefits, it would not be possible to know which agents (or combination of agents) were beneficial, and medical knowledge would not be advanced or treatment improved;

b)   the difficulty at (a) is compounded by the variation in the concentration of cannabinoids present in different preparations (although it seems that standardised preparations might be possible);

c)   the known toxic ingredients in cannabis smoke.

63   On cannabinoids (including apparently the cannabinols), the British Medical Association made the following recommendations, among others[30]:

    '1.   The World Health Organisation should advise the United Nations Commission on Narcotic Drugs to reschedule certain cannabinoids under the United Nations Convention on Psychotropic Substances, as in the case of dronabinol. In response the Home Office should alter the Misuse of Drugs Act accordingly.

    2.   In the absence of such action from the World Health Organisation, the Government should consider changing the Misuse of Drugs Act to allow the prescription of cannabinoids to patients with particular medical conditions not adequately controlled by existing treatments.'

64   The House of Lords Select Committee on Science and Technology said[31] that there was not enough rigorous scientific evidence to prove conclusively that cannabis itself has or has not medical value of any kind. Nevertheless the anecdotal evidence

---

[29]See pages 68 and 69 of report cited at footnote 16.
[30]See pages 78 and 79 of report cited at footnote 16.
[31]See paragraph 8.1 of report cited at footnote 3.

convinced them that cannabis almost certainly does have genuine medical applications, especially in treating multiple sclerosis. Because of the delays inherent in the system for licensing new medicines, they recommended that the Government should take steps to transfer cannabis and cannabis resin from Schedule 1 to the Misuse of Drugs Regulations 1985 to Schedule 2. This would permit doctors to prescribe an appropriate preparation of cannabis, albeit as an unlicensed medicine and on the named-patient basis, and allow doctors and pharmacists to supply the drug prescribed.

65   The Select Committee said that the principal reason for recommending that the law be changed was compassionate. Illegal medical use of cannabis was quite widespread and exposed patients and, in some cases, their carers to all the distress of criminal proceedings, with the possibility of serious penalties. As a secondary reason, the Committee mentioned that the law appeared to be being enforced inconsistently and sometimes with a very light hand. Some cases were not brought to court, and when they were, sentences were sometimes light or juries even refused to convict. They felt that this brought the law into disrepute and that, rather than enforce it more rigorously, it should be changed.

Our view

66   We appreciate the doubts of the British Medical Association over how to control and assess dosages of raw cannabis. But these seem to us insufficient reasons for preventing prescription where doctors, at their own risk on a named-patient basis, believe that their patients will benefit. Also, while understanding the reservations expressed by the British Medical Association and the House of Lords Select Committee about administration by smoking, this seems to us a very minor matter given the seriousness of the conditions for which prescription of cannabis seems likely to be beneficial.

67   We conclude that there is evidence that there are therapeutic benefits from the use of cannabis by people with certain serious illnesses and that these benefits outweigh any potential harm to themselves. We therefore agree with the House of Lords Select Committee that cannabis and cannabis resin, together with tincture and extracts not covered by the 1971 convention, should be transferred from Schedule 1 to Schedule 2 to the 1985 regulations. That would automatically ensure that doctors who prescribed such substances were not criminally liable. The same would apply to their patients in possession and doctors or pharmacists who supplied cannabis. Arrangements would need to be worked out for pharmacies to secure legitimate supplies of stocks, but that should not pose insuperable problems. We do not share the Government's anxiety about the capacity of GPs to withstand pressure for the prescription of cannabis. There is no evidence that this has been a problem where the prescription of heroin for pain control is concerned.

68   As the Government has rejected the House of Lords recommendations and it will be some years before a standard licensed cannabis product is available, we recommend that there should be a new defence of duress of circumstances on medical grounds for those accused of possessing, cultivating or supplying cannabis. We recommend that the burden be on the accused to prove the defence. This

approach would comply with our international obligations under the United Nations conventions and enable spurious defences to be rejected.

Arguments for and against change in the law

69   We are bound to accept that there is a risk that the changes in the law which we propose may lead to the use of cannabis by more people, some of whom may become dependent on it. But on the evidence of the current wide availability and use of the drug in the United Kingdom, and given the attitude of the public to the deterrent effect of the law, we do not think that the risk is significant. It is not possible to quantify it or to be sure that there will be an increase in use at all.

70   There may also be a risk of more people being dealt with more severely than at present if the Scottish system of fiscal fines is introduced in England and Wales as we recommend. Again we do not think that the risk is a serious one. The police are likely to be fairly selective in sending cannabis cases to the CPS for consideration of a fine. In any case, we envisage that statutory guidelines on these and on cautioning should define carefully the cases likely to be suitable for each disposal.

71   These are minor and largely speculative disadvantages compared to the real gains that we foresee from the changes that we recommend. They would lead to a law that fits better with public attitudes, and overcomes the present inhibition on accurate education about the dangers of cannabis, especially the long-term risks. It is this aspect of drug use which is usually absent from young people's assessment of harm. Better education should in turn lead to more responsible norms of cannabis taking, especially where driving is concerned.

72   A primary concern of ours is minimising the adverse, unnecessary and disproportionate criminal consequences for very large numbers of otherwise law-abiding, usually young, people. Our recommendations are intended to support the education, prevention and treatment elements of a broader health agenda, which itself reflects the relative risks of different drugs including cannabis. Our recommendations are not in breach of the United Nations Conventions. All of the present cannabis offences are being retained. The recommendations are in fact closer to the spirit of the conventions in taking an approach to personal consumption that is less punitive and more orientated towards health and education.

Our conclusions and recommendations on cannabis

73   Weighing the harm from cannabis against the costs of the current system of control leads us to the conclusion that cannabis is in the wrong class in the MDA, both as a reflection of its dangers relative to other drugs and in respect of the penalties attached to its possession, cultivation and supply. International comparisons indicate that different approaches are possible within the United Nations Conventions, and do not pose significant risk of worsening the situation.

74   As long as cannabis is illegal and so widely used, it will be the drug that occurs most frequently in all enforcement activities against drug misuse, whatever their

objective. Inevitably, cannabis offences and especially offences of cannabis possession, will dominate the operation of the law in statistical terms, reflecting very large numbers of arrests, prosecutions and criminal records. Despite this expense of time and resources by the courts, and especially the police, there is little evidence of the law's effectiveness as a deterrent. While we have accepted that the police need to retain the powers of stop and search conferred by the MDA, we have seen no evidence to persuade us that they need to retain the power of arrest following the discovery of cannabis, whether as a result of stop and search or other operations.

75   There can be no doubt that, in implementing the law, the present concentration on cannabis weakens respect for the law. We have encountered a wide sense of unease, indeed scepticism, about the present control regime in relation to cannabis. It inhibits accurate education about the relative risks of different drugs including the risks of cannabis itself. It gives large numbers of otherwise law-abiding people a criminal record. It inordinately penalises and marginalises young people for what might be little more than youthful experimentation. It bears most heavily on young people in the streets of inner cities who are also more likely to be poor and members of minority ethnic communites. The evidence strongly indicates that the current law and its operation creates more harm than the drug itself.

76   We see our recommendations as the first steps of an incremental process. The aims of this process are to achieve less coercive but more effective ways of reducing the harms of cannabis, and to bring those harms and the harms of the law into a better balance.

77   Our recommendations on the law on cannabis and its implementation are:

   i)   Cannabis should be transferred from Class B to Class C of Schedule 2 of the MDA and cannabinol and its derivatives should be transferred from Class A to Class C.

   ii)   The possession of cannabis should not be an imprisonable offence. As a consequence, it will no longer be an arrestable offence in England and Wales under section 24 of PACE, and arrests will only be possible under section 25 of PACE where there are identification or preventative grounds.

   iii) Prosecution of offences of cannabis possession should be the exception and only then should an offence, resulting in a conviction, incur a criminal record. An informal warning, a formal caution, a reprimand or warning in the case of those aged 17 or under, or a fixed out-of-court fine should be the normal range of sanctions.

   iv)   The cultivation of small numbers of cannabis plants for personal use should be a separate offence from production and should be treated in the same way as possession of cannabis, being neither arrestable nor imprisonable and attracting the same range of sanctions. Cultivation of cannabis for personal use under section 6 and production under section 4 should be mutually exclusive offences.

   v)   The maximum penalty for trafficking offences for Class C drugs, including cannabis, should be 7 years imprisonment and/or an unlimited fine. This is broadly in line with those European countries which we have studied and somewhat higher than most of them. Cannabis trafficking offences would, like all such offences, continue to attract the confiscation powers of the Drug Trafficking Act 1994.

vi) Permitting or suffering people to smoke cannabis on premises which one occupies or manages should no longer be an offence under section 8 of the Misuse of Drugs Act 1971.

vii) Statutory sentencing guidelines should include vicinity to schools, psychiatric services and prisons as aggravating factors for the purposes of sentencing for trafficking offences.

viii) Cannabis and cannabis resin should be moved from Schedule 1 to Schedule 2 of the MDA Regulations thereby permitting supply and possession for medical purposes. If there is to be any delay in adopting this recommendation pending the development of a plant with consistent dosage, we recommend a defence of duress of circumstance on medical grounds for those accused of the possession, cultivation or supply of cannabis.

Chapter Eight: Treatment And The Law

Introduction

1   One of the important features of the past two decades has been the gradual accumulation of evidence from research, first in the United States and more recently from the United Kingdom, showing that treatment is effective in reducing drug use and the criminal activity related to it, and that it is cost-effective. There is also research evidence to suggest that treatment can be effective even if there is some coercion involved. In this chapter we review this evidence and consider the various ways in which the law can best promote treatment responses to drug use. We also consider two issues that are linked to treatment provision: the extent to which doctors should be licensed to prescribe particular drugs and the changes needed to the Regulations governing prescriptions by doctors and their dispensing by pharmacists.

The case for treatment within the criminal justice system

2   A series of now well-known studies from the United States have compared the costs and benefits of treatment programmes. The U.S. Treatment Outcome Prospective Study[1] estimated that for every $6 spent on methadone maintenance programmes, benefits worth $13 were achieved. A RAND Corporation study[2] put the benefits from treatment at $7 for every $1 spent and found that treatment programmes for cocaine users achieved break-even savings, unlike other strategies for reducing the demand for and supply of cocaine.

3   In this country the largest such study is the National Treatment Outcome Research Study. It monitors the progress of 1,075 clients in four forms of treatment - two residential and two community. The residential treatments are specialist inpatient and rehabilitation programmes. The two community approaches are methadone maintenance and methadone reduction programmes. Broadly speaking, the residential treatment programmes are abstinence based, while the community programmes aim to reduce drug-taking and its related risk behaviours in the interests of harm reduction.

4   Impressive improvements in drug-taking and other behaviour as well as in psychological and physical health are indicated by the results of monitoring thus far[3]. At the one year mark, abstinence rates for the use of heroin and non-prescribed methadone had doubled. Injecting and sharing of equipment had more than halved. There was a marked reduction, albeit self-reported, in criminal activity, of which shoplifting was the most commonly reported crime before treatment. Burglary had come down by 87%. The researchers estimated that, for every £1 spent on treatment, £3 was saved to the criminal justice system.

5   At the two year follow-up[4] these improvements were substantially maintained, in abstinence rates, frequency and quantity of use and injecting. Rates of acquisitive

---

[1]Cited in D. Gerstein, *The Effectiveness of Drug Treatment.* In C. O'Brien and J. Jaffe (eds.) Addictive States, New York, Raven Press 1993.
[2]C. Rydell and S. Everingham, *Controlling Cocaine: Supply versus demand programs,* RAND Drug Policy Research Center, Santa Monica 1994.
[3]M. Gossop, J. Marsden, D. Stewart. *NTORS at One Year: Changes in substance use, health and criminal behaviours one year after intake.,* London, Department of Health 1998.
[4]M. Gossop, D. Stewart, A. Rolfe and J. Marsden *NTORS: Two Year Outcomes. Changes in Substance Use, Health and Crime.,* London, Department of Health 1999.

crime approximately halved, with large reductions in the number of offences. There were also large decreases in drug supply offences, with only 13% of residential and 10% of community clients still involved in selling drugs compared with 36% and 24% at intake. While many questions remain to be resolved by the research, it leaves no doubt about the cost-effectiveness of treatment.

6   Arrest referral schemes put people arrested by the police in touch with drug treatment and advice services. Where these schemes provide drugs workers at police stations and support after referral, research has shown that they can reduce drug use and drug-related crime. Evaluations of schemes in Brighton, Derby and Southwark are described in a recent report[5]. Most of the sample reported reductions in their drug use at the 6-8 month follow up. Just over a quarter said that they were no longer using any form of illicit drug and just over a third that they were no longer using illicit opiates or stimulants. The number of those who injected drugs also fell significantly. Falls were also reported in expenditure on drugs and in the number of crimes committed. The researchers estimated that the savings to both the health services and the criminal justice system were significant. A later study[6] found that the benefits of arrest referral lasted in over a quarter of cases well into the second year following referral. This study also found that probation orders with treatment conditions attached had been particularly effective in retaining offenders in treatment and reducing their expenditure on drugs.

7   The Government's 10-Year Strategy for Tackling Drugs Misuse recognises the strength of the accumulating evidence on treatment effectiveness, and places a strong emphasis on the role of treatment in tackling drug misuse and, in particular, on its role in protecting communities from drug-related antisocial and criminal behaviour. It sees the criminal justice system as having an important function in identifying drug users not receiving treatment services, facilitating their access to those services and ensuring their participation and continuance in treatment through formal and informal sanctions.

8   We welcome this emphasis on treatment in the national strategy and accept the rationale for using the criminal justice system to channel drug misusing offenders into treatment. We also welcome the opportunity this provides for offenders who are problem drug users who have not been reached by services. It is an approach which needs, however, to be tempered by several important caveats.

9   Drug misuse is first and foremost a public and individual health problem and second a crime problem. Although the scale of their offending is large, it is only a small minority of drug users, even problem drug users, who commit crime. It is important that diversion via the criminal justice system does not distort the use of current services and the allocation of future resources at the expense of the majority of problem drug users who do not commit crime and who can be prevented from committing crime by early access to treatment.

Resources

10   This is a particular danger when there is a shortage of services as at present. Long waiting lists are reported even though the evidence suggests that only a minority of

---

[5]M. Edmunds, T. May, I. Hearnden, M. Hough. *Arrest referral: Emerging lessons from research,* Drugs Prevention Initiative Paper 23, London, Home Office 1998.
[6]M. Edmonds, M. Hough, P. Turnbull, T. May. *Doing Justice to Treatment: referring offenders to drug services,* DPAS Paper 2, London, Home Office 1999.

problem drugs users are in touch with services. Moreover, research has found that two in three problem users identified by arrest referral workers are not currently in touch with drug services[7].

11   The first Annual Report on the national strategy, covering the year 1998/99, clearly recognises that 'the supply of effective treatment services is failing to match demand'[8] and that there has actually been a loss of residential treatment provision over the last few years. Significant additional resources have been allocated for drug services over the next few years to increase provision and speed of access. Nevertheless, in the short to medium term this situation means that capacity will not meet demand and the balance between the different routes to treatment needs to be carefully monitored. We see the need for a very substantial reallocation of resources and particularly the need to increase the provision of services for adolescents, women, people from minority ethnic communities and people with mental health problems.

12   Chronic shortage of drug services also means that the criminal justice system's capacity to divert offenders to treatment will often be a lottery – whether an offender receives treatment or punishment may depend on the availability of services. If, as is often the case, treatment services concentrate on heroin misuse, heroin users will be the chief beneficiaries of diversion or of sentences which include treatment while other problem users will not benefit in the same way. There is a further danger which must be guarded against in the enthusiasm to provide treatment via the law. This is the ratchet effect of failure in treatment resulting in a more punitive response than would have been the case without it.

13   Above all, it must be remembered that the key elements of effective treatment are the same whether delivered within the criminal justice system or not. It is important that treatment through the criminal justice system should encompass them. This means identifying those drug users for whom treatment is the appropriate response, getting them into treatment quickly and for long enough, providing incentives to achieve this, addressing the social as well as the clinical needs, and ensuring the provision of aftercare and support on which the success of rehabilitation depends. We have reservations about the possibility of delivering these objectives in prison, especially during periods of remand or short sentences. Where a response is sought to problem drug use, as opposed to the crime related to it, treatment in prison seems to us always likely to be a second-best option, and sentencers should not be attracted to it as a solution.

14   More far-reaching research is needed to provide a better understanding of the precise dynamics and causal links in the drugs-crime relationship, and better evidence about the factors that influence the effects of treatment. There is a particular need to evaluate the cost-effectiveness of different interventions, whether involving treatment or not. This is necessary to inform future decisions on what seems to us an unsatisfactory distribution of overall drugs expenditure, **with 62% going on enforcement and only 13% on treatment services.**

---

[7]Page 8 of the report cited at footnote 6.
[8]The United Kingdom Anti-drugs Co-ordinator, *First Annual Report and National Plan,* Cabinet Office 1999. Page 8.

15   Subject to these reservations, we consider in the following paragraphs the treatment responses within the criminal justice system. In particular, we consider whether the criminal law, which was not designed to further treatment objectives, is sufficiently flexible to encompass them or whether changes are needed. These are not issues specific to the MDA but affect many offenders against it.

Treatment as part of the criminal justice process

Caution-plus

16   'Caution-plus' schemes provide an alternative to prosecution. They are not statutory, although the Government's 10-year strategy, in promoting them, implies that they are. These schemes vary between police force areas. It is therefore difficult to describe them in terms of a model that will necessarily be recognisable throughout England and Wales and Northern Ireland. (There are no cautions or caution-plus schemes in Scotland but referral to treatment agencies in lieu of prosecution takes place there too[9]. The essential feature is that, as part of the decision to caution, the offender agrees to seek treatment or counselling or is given appropriate information when the caution is administered on where to obtain such assistance.

17   Under the Police and Criminal Evidence Act 1984 (PACE), the police are in general required, if they are going to charge a person with a criminal offence, to do so as soon as they have sufficient evidence to support the charge. If they do not bring the charge at that point, they may be precluded from doing so later. Moreover, once the charge is brought, there can be no further questioning about the offence except in carefully defined circumstances.

18   Arguably, therefore, as soon as the evidence to support the charge becomes available, interviews should not be prolonged or further questioning take place to discuss whether or not offenders are prepared to seek treatment. Also, charges cannot be delayed until offenders produce, or fail to produce, proof that they have entered a programme of treatment or counselling. There are no powers to enforce any conditions attached to a caution and Home Office guidance warns the police not to imply in any way that a caution is in any sense a reward for agreeing to seek treatment. It follows that the police are also powerless to follow up offenders in order to ensure that any undertakings given by them are carried out.

19   These difficulties also apply to arrest referral schemes in general and we set out our recommendations below for changing the law in order to remove the present doubts over whether they can operate lawfully. As far as caution-plus is concerned, it seems to us sensible that a statutory framework and guidelines governing the conditions that may be attached to a caution should be part of the same legislation that, as we have recommended earlier[10], would put cautioning of those over 17 on a statutory basis[11]. That should significantly improve the ability of the police service to contribute to such schemes. We do not, however, envisage that every police force would operate caution-plus schemes on a uniform basis across the country, at least initially. Much will depend on the available resources and the extent to which such schemes, demanding as they do cooperation with a variety of other agencies,

[9]See paragraph 23 below.
[10]Chapter Six, paragraph 31.
[11]For those under 18 cautions will be replaced from April 2000 by the new system of reprimands and warnings introduced by the Crime and Disorder Act 1998. See Chapter Six, paragraphs 22 to 24.

have been worked out. Nor do we wish to see such arrangements used in cases which are satisfactorily dealt with now by a normal caution. That should be avoided by suitably worded guidance under the new statutory scheme.

Arrest referral

20   'Caution-plus' is a variant of schemes known generally as 'arrest referral'. Its main effect is to keep the offender out of the courts (and in England and Wales the case will not be referred to the prosecuting authority). Other arrest referral schemes are designed to encourage an offender to obtain help and advice while the criminal justice process of charge, bail, trial and sentence continues. They fall into two basic categories. In one the custody officer simply hands out information, for example a list of names, addresses and telephone numbers of local drugs services, leaving it to the arrested person to make contact with the services. In the second type of scheme drugs counsellors work in close cooperation with the police, usually with direct access to suspects in the police station and sometimes continuing to support those who enter treatment as a result of arrest referral. All schemes have to avoid offering the possibility of dropping or not preferring charges as an inducement to compliance. None are on a statutory basis.

21   The main difficulties faced by arrest referral schemes have already been described in our discussion of caution-plus. The difficulties of reconciling them with the demands of PACE are more serious given that some candidates clearly suitable for arrest referral may be denying the offences for which they have been arrested. It seems to us that the present restrictions unduly inhibit the ability of the law to support the Government's declared policy in favour of caution-plus and arrest referral schemes. We therefore make the following recommendations, subject to the reservation that we do not regard the benefits of treatment as sufficient reason for providing a power of arrest where that would not otherwise be justified:

i)   It should be made clear (by amending PACE if necessary) that further questioning to establish willingness to undergo treatment is permissible after the evidence to support a charge has been obtained. But this should take place only with the suspect's agreement. If further evidence of criminal offences then emerges, the full procedures relating to interviews of suspects should again apply.

ii)   The relevant PACE Code should be redrafted so as to draw a clear distinction between questions designed to establish guilt and questions designed to establish an offender's willingness to undergo treatment. The Code could then go on to lay down at which point each type of questioning could take place – there are already similar exceptions in the present Code.

iii) The police should be given statutory powers to attach conditions to a caution, including the power to charge the offender with the original offence if the conditions are not met.

iv)   The power to attach conditions should be supported by statutory guidelines making it clear what sort of conditions are permissible and how compliance should be assessed.

v)   The police should be given powers to release offenders on police bail while arrangements for treatment are made. If such arrangements are not made the offender could be charged for the offence.

Pre-sentence

22   Although inducements must not be held out to defendants to agree to undergo treatment in the hope of charges being dropped, it is possible that as a result of arrest referral evidence will emerge before trial of factors that may indicate that the prosecution should be dropped in the public interest. Arrangements therefore need to be in place to ensure that any such information is passed to the Crown Prosecution Service for consideration. The main source of such information is likely to be the probation service.

23   In Scotland there are various diversion schemes, with the participation of social work departments and other agencies, for offenders whose behaviour appears to be the result of some underlying cause such as alcohol or drug dependence. These schemes operate on the basis of either deferral or waiver of prosecution. The offender's consent is required for participation in such schemes.

Sentence

Community orders

24   If they find offenders guilty, the courts may make one of a variety of orders (known collectively as community orders) which will result in them being supervised by the probation service. These include probation orders, community service orders and combination orders. Since the Criminal Justice Act 1991 the courts have been able to attach to probation orders a requirement that the offender undergoes treatment. Where this is not done, it is still open to the probation officer, where treatment seems to be needed, to encourage the offender to seek it.

25   5,149 people found guilty of drugs offences were sentenced to probation or supervision in 1997. 1,970 of them were required under the 1991 Criminal Justice Act to undergo drug or alcohol treatment as part of the order. No information is available on the numbers of people encouraged by probation officers to seek treatment in the absence of a specific requirement attached to the order. We believe that attaching treatment conditions to probation orders remains a credible option for a wide range of drugs offences. There is now emerging evidence of their effectiveness[12]. As we have already said in our discussion of possession offences[13], it may be possible to use them more often. As we also point out in the same context, the removal of this sanction under the Crime and Disorder Act 1998 where drug treatment and testing orders become available is a mistake which should be reversed at the earliest opportunity.

Drug treatment and testing orders

26   Drug treatment and testing orders may be made from autumn 2000 under section 61 of the Crime and Disorder Act 1998. The court may make an order in any case where the sentence is not mandatory. Orders may last from three months to three

---

[12]See paragraph 6.
[13]Chapter Five, paragraphs 17 and 18.

years. They can only be made if the court has been notified by the Secretary of State that arrangements for implementing them are available in the area. The court has to be satisfied before making the order that the offender 'is dependent on or has a propensity to misuse drugs and that this dependency or propensity is such as requires and may be susceptible to treatment'.

27 The order may specify who is to administer or supervise the treatment and where and whether the treatment is to be residential or non-residential. Apart from this the court has no powers to specify the nature of the treatment. The order can only be imposed if the offender expresses his willingness to comply with its requirements. It is accompanied by arrangements for testing for the presence of drugs as the supervision progresses. Offenders who do not stay the course because they fail these tests or in other ways risk more severe penalties.

28 The orders are not primarily directed against drugs offenders as such; they were created to break the links between drug misuse and other types of offending. As the Home Office guidance to pilot areas makes clear, the orders are primarily designed for those convicted of acquisitive crimes committed in order to obtain money to buy drugs. The guidance notes, however, that 'offenders convicted of drug supply who are themselves habitual misusers, and are otherwise suitable for a community sentence...should also be considered'. We believe that this general approach to the use of the new order is correct; it is most appropriate for those whose offences are drug-related but not drugs offences as such.

29 The interim findings on three pilot areas where drug treatment and testing orders have been introduced were published in late 1999[14]. It is too soon to draw firm conclusions particularly as the 55 offenders interviewed, over half of whom had been convicted of shoplifting, had only been on the order for one month. The findings show substantial reductions in the amount spent on drugs and in acquisitive crime, although they also show a high level of failure in meeting the conditions of the order. There were large differences between sentencers in their expectations of the speed with which results can be delivered. If greater consistency is to be achieved clear guidelines will be needed on when breach proceedings are appropriate and also to ensure a better match between treatment and the individual's needs.

Controls over prescribing

30 The MDA and its associated Regulations govern what can be prescribed and by whom. They also regulate many other aspects of the distribution, production, storage and dispensing of controlled drugs.

31 Section 10 of the MDA enables the Secretary of State to make Regulations governing:

 i) safe custody;

 ii) the documentation of transactions and the keeping of records;

 iii) packaging and labelling;

 iv) transport;

---

[14]P. Turnbull. *Drug Treatment and Testing Orders Interim Evaluation*. Research, Development and Statistics Directorate Research Findings No. 106, London, Home Office 1999.

v)   methods of destruction;

vi)   prescriptions;

vii) notification by doctors of persons suspected of addiction (this is not a current requirement but the power remains);

viii) licensing of doctors to prescribe certain drugs to addicts.

32   Sections 12 – 16 of the MDA give the Home Secretary powers to give directions withdrawing from individual doctors, vets, or pharmacists their authority to possess, prescribe, administer, manufacture, compound and supply specified controlled drugs. These powers are subject to various rights of appeal to tribunals, advice from professional panels and other procedures.

Doctors

33   Under regulations made under the MDA, a doctor cannot prescribe heroin, cocaine or dipipanone to addicts unless he has been licensed to do so by the Home Secretary, or the drugs are supplied or prescribed for the treatment of organic disease or injury.

34   Other controlled drugs can be prescribed by any doctor to a problem drug user. The evidence suggests there are wide divergences in prescribing practice, particularly between private and NHS prescribing. A survey of prescription records[15,16], has shown that prescriptions from private doctors were more likely to be for larger amounts, at higher doses, to be dispensed in weekly, fortnightly or monthly instalments, and that the drugs concerned, particularly in the case of methadone, were more likely to be in injectable form. Although the MDA lays down an independent tribunal system for dealing with doctors who prescribe irresponsibly, it is cumbersome and inflexible and has not been used for the last three years.

35   It seems to us that private prescribing to problem drug users is always likely to raise particular difficulties, being based as it is on the payment of a fee by patients who will often have very limited incomes. Such patients will always wish to minimise both the number of consultations and the number of prescriptions, for which they also have to pay. The risks to patients of large prescriptions for relatively long periods dispensed at one time are obvious and underlined by the increase in methadone-related deaths, from 230 in 1993 to 421 in 1997. There is also evidence[17] that drugs from such prescriptions, particularly of injectable methadone and amphetamine, are spilling out onto the illicit market in significant quantities. The Advisory Council on the Misuse of Drugs expressed its concern about the private treatment of problem drug takers as long ago as 1982[18].

36   There is a strong case, that in our view needs urgent consideration, for extending the licensing system under the MDA so that doctors in private practice and NHS doctors who prescribe privately have to be licensed if they wish to prescribe any Class A drug to an addict. Such licences should be based on criteria which include the doctor's training and links to specialist support. The existing tribunal system should be abolished. A national register of private prescriptions should be set up,

[15]J. Strang, J. Sheridan and N. Barber. 'Prescribing injectable and oral methadone to opiate addicts: results from the 1995 national postal survey of community pharmacies in England and Wales.' *British Medical Journal*, 313, pages 270-272, 1996.
[16]J. Strang and J. Sheridan. 'National and regional characteristics of methadone prescribing in England and Wales; local analyses from the 1995 national survey of community pharmacies.' *Journal of Substance Misuse*, 3, pages 240-246, 1998.
[17]M. Edmunds, M. Hough and N. Urquia. *Tackling Local Drugs Markets* Police Research Group. Crime Detection and Prevention Series Paper 80, London, Home Office 1996.
[18]*Treatment and Rehabilitation*. London, Department of Health and Social Security 1982.

probably by an extension of the present NHS system to include private prescriptions, and arrangements made to scrutinise and monitor them. The licensing system and rights of appeal should be under the control of Directors of Public Health, who are also best placed to judge local needs for availability of services for problem drug users.

37   We think that the abolition of the requirement for doctors to notify their addict patients to the Chief Medical Officer at the Home Office has created a new obstacle to responsible prescribing for problem drug users. There is now no national information system to provide general practitioners and other prescribers with up-to-date information on prescribing, in particular of Class A drugs to problem drug users, so as to minimise the risks of double prescribing. This gap needs to be filled and we support the recommendation by the British Medical Association in 1997[19] for 'a national, comprehensive, confidential information system...to provide up-to-date prescribing information on individuals, accessible to general practitioners and other prescribers, available out-of-hours, including weekends.'

Pharmacists

38   As for the other issues covered by sections 10 - 16 of the Act, the Inquiry has been sent a report with 59 recommendations by the Royal Pharmaceutical Society of Great Britain. The overall aim is to remedy the practical problems that community pharmacists face because the current Misuse of Drugs Regulations make it very difficult to manage efficiently the provision of instalment dispensing services to drug misusers. Pharmacists face many difficulties with customers, especially when they present incorrectly written prescriptions. They therefore need a more relevant legal framework that allows them to exercise professional judgement when dealing with trivial or clerical errors or omissions in prescriptions for controlled drugs. We urge the government to give urgent and sympathetic consideration to this report. It is, for example, a curious anomaly, and one that adds to the risks to patients, that in England and Wales drug misusers may obtain only a limited range of drugs[20] in instalments. In Scotland, however, doctors may use one form to prescribe any drug in instalments. We support the recommendation that arrangements should be standardised throughout the United Kingdom to enable patients to obtain medicines other than Schedule 2 controlled drugs, for example amphetamines, temazepam and the other benzodiazepines, in instalments.

39   We draw particular attention to the following recommendations (the numbering is ours, not that of the report) made by the Royal Pharmaceutical Society which fall within the remit of our Inquiry:

    i)   the rules for prescribers' handwriting exemptions on controlled drugs prescriptions should be reviewed by the Home Office

    ii)   pharmacists should be able to amend instalment prescriptions after contacting the prescriber

    iii) the Misuse of Drugs Regulations relating to instalment dispensing need updating and amendment to facilitate action when a client fails to collect

---

[19] *The Misuse of Drugs*, Amsterdam, Harwood Academic Publishers 1997. Recommendation 12, page 146.
[20] These include heroin, cocaine and most of the drugs in Schedule 2 to the Misuse of Drugs Regulations 1985 but not the drugs in other Schedules, notably the benzodiazepines.

iv) the Regulations should be amended to allow an instalment scheduled for supply on a day when the pharmacy will be closed to be supplied on the preceding day

v) there should be a review of the legality of dispensing prescriptions for methadone mixture where the client asks for variation from the formulation prescribed

vi) the maximum number of days' treatment on any prescription for drug misusers should be 14 days

vii) the facility for instalment prescribing in England and Wales should be extended, as is the case in Scotland, beyond Schedule 2 drugs so that it is possible to dispense instalments of other drugs liable to misuse such as benzodiazepines.

Note of Reservation by Denis O'Connor

I would like to record my enduring reservations on the workability of the recommendations and proposals that relate to cannabis.

There are consequences of reclassifying cannabis with respect to removing the power of arrest for possession that will create real problems for operational officers. These include: the workability of any confiscation procedure; decision making as to whether it is a case of supply as opposed to possession; and the need to accommodate criminal justice processes and documentation associated with any caution or any other criminal justice outcome.

We have discussed (see Chapter 5, paragraphs 27-32) the impact that this might have on street activity involving drugs, not only drug markets but also the associated anti-social behaviour that concerns the public so much. There is a potential adverse effect here which ideally needs to be properly scoped.

These issues are not entirely insurmountable but do need to be addressed if we are to have a coherent approach to this problem.

DENIS O'CONNOR

Summary of Recommendations

Recommendation Number	The Present Situation	Chapter Two: Paragraph
1	The information and research base should be given renewed attention. In particular: i) routine statistics should be improved to ensure that gaps in our understanding of the scale, nature and extent of drug use are reduced; and ii) enforcement and treatment policies should be evaluated thoroughly.	77
	Classes and Schedules	**Chapter Three: Paragraph**
2	The present classification of drugs in the MDA should be reviewed to take account of modern developments in medical, sociological and scientific knowledge.	7
3	The main classification criterion should continue to be that of dangerousness.	7
4	The chronic health risks from each drug should be kept under continuous review.	11
5	The model of three classes offered by the MDA should be retained.	26
6	There should be clear criteria for the future to govern additions to, and transfers between, the classes.	27 & 38
7	Ecstasy and related compounds should be transferred from Class A to Class B.	30 & 36 i)
8	LSD should be transferred from Class A to Class B.	36 ii)
9	Cannabinols such as d-9 THC should be transferred from Class A to Class C.	31 & 36 iii)
10	The Government should encourage the development and manufacture of benzodiazepines in combination with an antagonist, such as flumazenil, that would block the 'high' when used intravenously but would not affect the therapeutic response when used orally.	32

Recommendation	Classes and Schedules	Chapter Three: Paragraph
11	Doctors should be encouraged to prescribe the less abused benzodiazepines and non-benzodiazepine alternatives.	32
12	Buprenorphine (except when in combination with naloxone) should be transferred from Class C to Class B.	33 & 36 iv)
13	Herbal cannabis and cannabis resin should be transferred from Class B to Class C.	36 v)
14	The Advisory Council for the Misuse of Drugs should continue to be the body that has the statutory responsibility for considering and making recommendations to Ministers on the classification of new drugs and for keeping the existing classes under review.	46
15	Future reports from the Council should clearly state its methods and findings on such matters.	46
16	The Government should study the United States and the Netherlands systems with a view to establishing an effective early warning system in this country.	49
	Trafficking Offences	**Chapter Four: Paragraph**
17	The Government should set up a detailed and in-depth examination of the relationship between the Misuse of Drugs Act 1971 and the Customs and Excise Management Act 1979.	15
18	There should be a separate offence of dealing, the main ingredient of which would be the pattern of activity of illicitly transacting business in drugs. It should be capable of being charged as a continuing offence.	27
19	The new offence of dealing should be designated a trafficking offence for the purposes of the Drug Trafficking Act 1994.	28
20	It should be a defence for a person accused of supply or possession with intent to supply to prove that he was a member of a small social group who supplied or intended to supply a controlled drug (other than a drug of Class A) to another member or other members of that group believing that he was acting, or had acted, on behalf of the group, which shared a common intention to use the drug for personal consumption. This defence would only	30 & 35

Recommendation Number	Trafficking Offences	Chapter Four: Paragraph
20 continued	apply where the court was satisfied that the amount or value of the controlled drug was consistent with personal use within the group concerned.	
21	Maximum penalties for trafficking offences under the MDA and CEMA should be amended as shown in Table 4.3 on page 67.	39
22	The penalties for other trafficking offences, such as money laundering and illicit traffic in precursor chemicals, should be separately considered and, if necessary in order to achieve consistency, brought into line.	39
23	Drugs offences should be designated as a relevant category of offence for the purposes of sections 80 and 81 of the Crime and Disorder Act 1998 and guidelines proposed by the Sentencing Advisory Panel for consideration by the Court of Appeal.	41
24	The factors set out in Chapter Four, paragraph 43, should be taken account of in such guidelines.	43
25	Before further consideration is given to confiscation of assets under civil law, steps should be taken to strengthen and make maximum use of the existing criminal law procedures.	51 and 52
26	The responsibility for enforcement of confiscation orders should lie with the crown court not with the magistrates' courts.	53
27	The time limit set for payment of the amount named in a confiscation order should be that which seems reasonable to the court having looked into the circumstances and heard and tested the arguments of prosecution and defence.	54
28	The recommendations in the Home Office consultation paper for improving the effectiveness of the present criminal law system of confiscation should be followed up except where they are overtaken by our recommendations, particularly number 26.	55
29	The new national confiscation agency proposed by the Home Office should be set up with the overriding remit of ensuring that the present criminal confiscation machinery, reformed as we propose, achieves full efficiency.	56

Recommendation Number	Trafficking Offences	Chapter Four: Paragraph
30	A considerable investment in recruitment and training of people with the requisite skills should be made in most branches of the criminal justice system, in particular the police, prosecution, and courts (including the judges).	57
31	It should be possible for the courts to order the forfeiture of property other than land seized by the police which was clearly about to be used in the commission of a further offence.	59
	Non-Trafficking Offences	**Chapter Five: Paragraph**
32	The law should take full advantage of the leeway left by the United Nations conventions to deal with the less serious situations in a non-punitive way.	11
33	A maximum penalty of imprisonment albeit on a lower scale should be retained for Class A drugs.	13
34	In the case of Class B and Class C drugs, the present custodial penalties should be removed and the courts should develop further the non-custodial responses already available to them.	14
35	As soon as legislative opportunity permits, the progressive repeal of the ability of the courts to attach treatment conditions to probation orders in drugs cases should be reversed.	18
36	The maximum penalties for possession offences should be as set out in Table 5.2 on page 79.	19
37	Arrestability under section 24 of PACE should be retained for possession offences involving Class A and Class B drugs.	32
38	Possession of Class C drugs is not an arrestable offence at present. This situation would not change when cannabis is transferred to Class C.	32
39	In Scotland the present powers of detention should be retained for possession of Class A and Class B drugs but should not be extended to Class C drugs when cannabis is transferred there.	33
40	The police should develop procedures for properly recording and documenting drug seizures that take place on the streets.	34

Recommendation Number	Non-Trafficking Offences	Chapter Five: Paragraph
41	Paragraphs (a) and (b) of section 8 (knowingly permitting or suffering supply and production) should be retained subject to redrafting designed to make it clear that the main aim is to deter those who wilfully allow others to produce or supply controlled drugs.	41 and 42
42	'Wilfully' should be defined as meaning 'not caring whether the unlawful production or supply takes place or not'.	41
43	A person should not be regarded as acting wilfully merely by reason of his failure to disclose confidential records or material in respect of the persons in his care.	41
44	Section 8 should be extended to include the new offence of dealing recommended at 18 above.	42
45	The maximum custodial penalty on indictment for premises offences involving Class B drugs should be reduced from 14 years to 7.	42
46	Paragraphs (c) and (d) of section 8 (knowingly permitting or suffering premises to be used for preparing opium or for smoking cannabis or opium) should be repealed.	44
47	It should be a condition of their licences that owners and managers of places of entertainment take measures for the safety of drug-takers.	45
48	Educational material about the main drugs and their risks, including the risks of driving, should be widely available at entertainment venues.	45
49	Section 9 of the MDA (offences relating to opium) should be repealed.	48
50	Section 9A of the MDA (paraphernalia) should be repealed.	53
51	The exemption for hypodermic syringes currently contained in section 9A should for the avoidance of doubt be inserted into section 19. It should be extended to other products.	53

Recommendation Number	Enforcement	Chapter Six: Paragraph
52	We welcome the recent amendments to Code A on strip searches.	8
53	The main need is for quality control and close monitoring of the outcomes of stop and search. The aim should be to have fewer stops and searches but a higher proportion of them with successful outcomes.	13
54	We support the Government's proposal that cautions, reprimands and warnings should become spent immediately, with the result that there would be no rehabilitation period for the purposes of the Rehabilitation of Offenders Act 1974.	20 and 24
55	Cautioning should become a statutory sanction, with guidelines laid down in regulations.	31
56	The fiscal fine system should be introduced in England and Wales for operation by the Crown Prosecution Service.	34
57	Out-of-court fines should only be used for cases that would otherwise be prosecuted and should not replace the caution in the kind of case for which cautions are used now. That might be ensured under statutory cautioning guidelines.	35
58	It should be made clear in legislation that cautions, reprimands, warnings, compounds and out-of-court fines should not be capable of being cited in court as evidence of the character either of the defendant or of a witness. Section 66(5) of the Crime and Disorder Act would need to be amended accordingly. A similar change is needed to CEMA's provisions on compounding.	36
59	Records of cautions, reprimands and warnings for drug possession offences should continue to be kept on the Police National Computer.	37
60	The Secretary of State should include information on drugs cautions, reprimands or warnings in criminal record certificates only in the most exceptional cases.	38

Recommendation Number	Cannabis	Chapter Seven: Paragraph
61	Cannabis should be transferred from Class B to Class C of Schedule 2 of the MDA and cannabinol and its derivatives should be transferred from Class A to Class C.	77 i)
62	The possession of cannabis should not be an imprisonable offence. As a consequence, it will no longer be an arrestable offence in England and Wales under section 24 of PACE, and arrests will only be possible under section 25 of PACE where there are identification or preventative grounds.	77 ii)
63	Prosecution of offences of cannabis possession should be the exception and only then should an offence, if it results in a conviction, incur a criminal record. An informal warning, a formal caution, a reprimand or warning in the case of those aged 17 or under, or a fixed out-of-court fine should be the normal range of sanctions.	77 iii)
64	The cultivation of small numbers of cannabis plants for personal use should be a separate offence from production and should be treated in the same way as possession of cannabis, being neither arrestable nor imprisonable and attracting the same range of sanctions. Cultivation of cannabis for personal use under section 6 and production under section 4 should be mutually exclusive offences.	41 and 77 iv)
65	The maximum penalty for trafficking offences for Class C drugs, including cannabis, should be 7 years imprisonment and/or an unlimited fine. Cannabis trafficking offences would, like all such offences, continue to attract the confiscation powers of the Drug Trafficking Act.	77 v)
66	Permitting or suffering people to smoke cannabis on premises which one owns or manages should no longer be an offence under section 8 of the MDA.	77 vi)
67	Statutory sentencing guidelines should include vicinity to schools, psychiatric services and prisons as aggravating factors for the purposes of sentencing for trafficking offences.	77 vii)
68	Cannabis and cannabis resin should be moved from Schedule 1 to Schedule 2 of the MDA Regulations thereby permitting supply and possession for medical purposes. If there is to be any delay in	79 viii)

Recommendation Number	Cannabis	Chapter Seven: Paragraph
68 continued	adopting this recommendation pending the development of a plant with consistent dosage, we recommend a defence of duress of circumstances on medical grounds for those accused of the possession, cultivation or supply of cannabis.	
	Treatment and the Law	**Chapter Eight: Paragraph**
69	We welcome the emphasis on treatment in the national strategy and accept the rationale for using the criminal justice system to channel drug misusing offenders into treatment.	8
70	There should be a very substantial reallocation of resources and particularly an increase in the provision of services for adolescents, women, people from minority ethnic communities and people with mental health problems.	11
71	Where a response is sought to problem drug use, as opposed to the crime related to it, treatment in prison should always be considered a second-best option, and sentencers should not be attracted to it as a solution.	13
72	More far-reaching research is needed to provide a better understanding of the precise dynamics and causal links in the drugs-crime relationship and better evidence about the factors that influence treatment effects. There is a particular need to evaluate the cost-effectiveness of different interventions, in order to inform future decisions on distribution of overall drugs expenditure.	14
73	A statutory framework and guidelines governing the conditions that may be attached to a caution should be part of the legislation that would put cautioning of those over 17 on a statutory basis. In particular: (i) the police should be given statutory powers to attach conditions to a caution, including the power to charge the offender with the original offence if the conditions are not met; (ii) the power to attach conditions should be supported by statutory guidelines making it clear what sort of conditions are permissible and how compliance should be assessed;	19 21 iii) 21 iv)

Recommendation Number	Treatment and the Law	Chapter Eight: Paragraph
73 *continued*	(iii) the police should be given powers to release offenders on police bail while arrangements for treatment are made; if such arrangements are not made the offender would be charged for the offence.	21 v)
74	It should be made clear (by amending PACE if necessary) that further questioning to establish willingness to undergo treatment is permissible after the evidence to support a charge has been obtained but that it should take place only with the suspect's agreement.	21 i)
75	The relevant PACE Code should be redrafted so as to draw a clear distinction between questions designed to establish guilt and questions designed to establish an offenderís willingness to undergo treatment. The Code could then go on to lay down at which point each type of questioning could take place.	21 iii)
76	Urgent consideration should be given to extending the licensing system under the MDA so that doctors in private practice and NHS doctors who prescribe privately have to be licensed if they wish to prescribe any Class A drug to an addict. Such licences should be based on criteria which include the doctor's training and links to specialist support.	36
77	A national register of private prescriptions should be set up and arrangements made to scrutinise and monitor them.	36
78	The existing tribunal system should be abolished.	36
79	The licensing system and rights of appeal should be under the control of Directors of Public Health.	36
80	We support the recommendation by the British Medical Association in 1997 for 'a national comprehensive, confidential information system... to provide up-to-date prescribing information on individuals, accessible to general practitioners and other prescribers, available out-of-hours, including weekends.'	37
81	We urge the government to give urgent and sympathetic consideration to the report of the Royal Pharmaceutical Society on services to drug misusers and in particular to the recommendations listed in paragraph 39 of chapter eight.	38

Appendix 1

The Members of the Inquiry

VISCOUNTESS RUNCIMAN D.B.E (Chairman)
Member of the Advisory Council on the Misuse of Drugs (1974-95) and Chairman of the Council's Criminal Justice Working Group; Chairman Mental Health Act Commission.

MRS ALISON CHESNEY*
Chief Executive, Cranstoun Drug Services (1992-1998)

MR RUDI FORTSON
Barrister at Law, Middle Temple and author of Misuse of Drugs and Drug Trafficking Offences.

MR JOHN HAMILTON QPM
Chief Constable, Fife Constabulary

MR SIMON JENKINS
Former Editor – The Times

PROFESSOR ALAN MAYNARD
Professor of Economics, University of York, Department of Economics and Related Studies.

MR LEONARD G. MURRAY**
Consultant, Levy and McRae Solicitors, Glasgow

PROFESSOR DAVID NUTT
Head, Mental Health and Psychopharmacology Unit, University of Bristol.

MR DENIS O'CONNOR QPM
Assistant Commissioner, Metropolitan Police Service

PROFESSOR GEOFFREY PEARSON
Wates Professor of Social Work, Goldsmiths' College.

MR IAN WARDLE
Chief Executive, Lifeline Project Limited.

PROFESSOR SIR BERNARD WILLIAMS
White's Professor of Moral Philosophy, University of Oxford (until 1996); Monroe Deutsch Professor of Philosophy, University of California – Berkeley.

MS ANNETTE ZERA
Principal, Tower Hamlets College, London.

* resigned 18 September 1998
** resigned 12 March 1998

Appendix 2

Terms of Reference

1 **Objectives**

1.1 To carry out an independent inquiry into the effectiveness of the relevant laws in order to assess options for legislative change and to provide the best informed possible revisions.

1.2 To encourage informed discussion among those who have a particular interest in the legislation, policy and practice addressing the misuse of drugs including legislators, policy-makers, the police, the medical and legal professions, statutory and voluntary service providers, teachers and academics.

1.3 More generally, to raise the level of public understanding and debate about the effectiveness of the relevant legislation, and the efficiency of its enforcement in achieving the aim of curbing the misuse of controlled drugs.

2 **Terms of Reference**

2.1 The Inquiry is asked to:

a. describe the purpose and intention behind the existing relevant legislation and place them in their historical context including the U.K. obligations under the United Nations drug conventions and to the European Union.

b. review and assess the current goals of drug misuse control.

c. assess the adequacy of the existing relevant legislation in meeting current needs.

d. compile a list of possible revisions to the existing relevant legislation pointing out agreement, conflicts and possible compromises if current legislation is found to be inadequate for some or all of the needs identified.

e. select the most cogent proposals for revision of the existing relevant legislation and examine the implications of their implementation.

2.2 The Inquiry is expected to decide its own mode of working, which may in particular include:

a. inviting written and/or oral testimony from individuals and organisations with particular experience of the issues under discussion;

b. determining the topics for the briefing and research papers to inform its deliberations;

c. commissioning those briefing and research papers necessary for its discussions;

d. convening seminars of experts in the field for discussion of the issues;

e. publishing briefing papers, research papers and reports as may be thought appropriate; and

f. devising a coordinated plan for the dissemination of the findings of the Inquiry.

3 **Operation of the Inquiry**

    3.1 The Inquiry has been established by the Police Foundation as an independent body and as such is not expected to represent the views of the Trustees or staff of the Foundation.

    3.2 The Police Foundation will provide the Inquiry with the resources essential to carrying out its work.

    3.3 The Police Foundation will serve as Secretariat of the Committee and take responsibility for:

        a. administrative coordination

        b. financial support

        c. commissioning the background papers or external studies required by the Committee.

        d. implementing the coordinated plan for disseminating the findings of the Inquiry.

    3.4 The Inquiry is expected to work in partnership with the Police Foundation in the overall administration of its work.

Appendix 3

Witnesses Who Provided Oral Evidence

Mr Peter Clay	Assistant Chief Constable and Director of Intelligence, National Criminal Intelligence Service
Mr Paul Cook	Consultant, European Monitoring Centre for Drugs and Drug Addiction
Ms Penny Cottan	Legal Advisor, Release
Mr Justice Peter Crane	Peterborough Crown Court
Mr Nicholas Dorn	Director of Research, Institute for the Study of Drug Dependence
Mr. Barry Dougal	Detective Superintendent, Strathclyde Police, Force Drugs Coordinator
Dr Michael Farrell	Senior Lecturer & Consultant Psychiatrist, National Addiction Centre
Mr Mike Franklin	Chair, Borough of Lambeth Community-Police Consultative Group
Mrs Christine Glover	Vice President, Royal Pharmaceutical Society of Great Britain; Chairman, Working Party on Pharmaceutical Services for Drug Misuse
Dr Michael Gossop	Project Director, , National Treatment Outcome Research Study, National Addiction Centre
Mr John Grieve	Deputy Assistant Commissioner, Metropolitan Police Service
Professor Michael Hough	South Bank University
Mr Michael Jay	Chairman, Drugs Policy Review Group
Mr A.D.J. Keizer	Head, Addiction Policy Division, Directorate of Mental Health and Addiction Policy, Ministry of Health, Welfare and Sport, The Netherlands.
Mr M Keybets	Brigadier, Police Department of Limburg Zuid, Maastricht, The Netherlands
Mr Simon Kirkham	Legal Advisor, Release
Mr Frans Koopmans	Director, Stichting "De Hoop", Dordrecht, The Netherlands

Mr Danny Kushlick	Director, Transform
Professor Malcolm Lader	Professor of Psychopharmacology and Chairman National Addiction Centre; Chairman, Technical Sub-Committee, Advisory Council on the Misuse of Drugs
Drs. Ed Leuw	Research and Documentation Centre, Ministry of Justice, The Netherlands
Mr Alan MacFarlane	Chief Inspector, Drugs Inspectorate, Home Office Action Against Drugs Unit
Professor Neil McKeganey	Chair, Centre for Drug Misuse Research, University of Glasgow
Mr Geoffrey Monaghan	Detective Sergeant, Intelligence Directorate, Drugs Unit, Metropolitan Police Service
Ms Arlene Mundle	Head, Race Harassment sub-Committee, Borough of Lambeth Community Police Consultative Group
Mr Roger Odd	Head, Practice Division, Royal Pharmaceutical Society of Great Britain
Professor Howard Parker	University of Manchester, Department of Social Work
Mr Colin Phillips	Chief Constable, Cumbria Constabulary and Chairman, Drugs Sub-Committee, Association of Chief Police Officers'
Mr Gregory Poulter	Deputy Director, Release
Professor John Strang	Director, National Addiction Centre
Mr Matthew Sutton	University of York, Centre for Health Economics
Mr Barry Taylor	Detective Superintendent, West Mercia Constabulary, Force Crime Manager
Dr David Thomas QC	Reader in Criminology, Institute of Criminology, Cambridge
Mr David Warren	Assistant Chief Constable, Avon and Somerset Constabulary and Secretary, Drugs Sub-Committee, Association of Chief Police Officers

Appendix 4

Individuals and Organisations Submitting Written Evidence

Individuals

Mr Neil N Ashton

Professor Mark R Baker

Dr A J Blowers

Mrs Mary Brett

Bro. Michael Carmichael OGS

Mr David R Copestake

Mr Roger Creasey

Mr Quentin England

Professor P B Fellgett FRS

Mr Paul Flynn MP

Mr Andy Francis

Mr J J Fraser

Ms Helen L Heathand

Anon. of Holywell, Flintshire

Mrs Hope Humphreys

Mr James Humphreys

Mr Mick Humphreys

Mr Richard Ives

Mr Kazim Khan

Rev. Kenneth Leach

Dr Alan John Lyons

Lord Mancroft

Dr John Marks

Mr Peter G B McNeill

Mr W M Peacock CBE

Mr Dennis Ramshaw

Mr K G Rickard

Mr I Robinson

Mr Al Sabbah

Mr Jonathon Sayers

Mr John N Wates

Mr David L Williams FRCGP

Mrs Joan Wollard

Organisations

Agapay

Association of Scottish Police Superintendents

Association of Chief Police Officers (Scotland)

Association of Chief Police Officers of England, Wales and Northern Ireland

Bedfordshire Drug Action Team

Birmingham Drug Action Team

Black Drug Workers Forum (North West)

BLWA (Association of Laboratory Supply Industry)

Bradford Drug and Alcohol Action Team

British Medical Association

Bury Drug Action Team

Cardiff Street Drugs Project

Cardinal Hume Centre

Catholic Bishops Conference of England and Wales

Church of England, Board of Social Responsibility

Committee of Vice Chancellors and Principals of the Universities of England
and Wales

Coroners Society of England and Wales

Crown Prosecution Service

D.I.D (Drugs in Deptford)

Daybreak Drug Abuse project

Diocese of Newcastle

Drugs Policy Review Group

Dudley Drug Action Team

Greater Manchester Drug Action Partnership

HM Customs and Excise

HM Inspector of Constabulary

Justices' Clerks' Society, England and Wales

Kaleidoscope Project

Kingston & Richmond Drug Action Team

Langley House Trust

Law Society

Liverpool Drug Action Team

Local Government Association

London Borough of Hillingdon Drug Education Team

Medical Research Council

Ministry of Sound

National Crime Squad (Eastern Area)

National Drug Prevention Alliance

National Pharmaceutical Association

National Union of Teachers

National Youth Agency

New Horizon Youth Centre

Northamptonshire Drug Action Team

Northumbria Police

Nottingham Drug Action Team

Police Federation of England and Wales

Rainbow Project

Re-Solv

Road Peace

Rotherham Drug Action Team

Royal College of Physicians

Royal Pharmaceutical Society of Great Britain

Scottish Police Federation

Shropshire Drug Action Team

South East London Probation Service

St Thomas Fund for the Homeless

Standing Conference on Drug Abuse

Stockport Drug Action Team

T.H.O.M.A.S. (Those on the Margins of Society)

The Depaul Trust

The Irish Bishops Conference

The Matthew Project

The Passage

The Stapleford Centre

THI and THI Macedon

Transform

Uxbridge Drug Action Team

Wakefield Drug Action Team

West Yorkshire Drug Prevention Team

Wirral Christian Drug Action

York Peace Centre

Yorkshire Television

Appendix 5

Main Events in Twentieth Century Drug Control

Sale of cocaine regulated under Poisons and Pharmacy Act 1908.

International Opium Convention 1912 (the Hague Convention) requires states party to it to limit the manufacture, trade and use of opiates to medical purposes; to close opium dens; to penalise unauthorised possession of opiates; and to prohibit their sale to unauthorised persons.

Defence of the Realm Act 1916 controls possession of cocaine.

Dangerous Drugs Act 1920 implements Hague Convention. Although principally concerned with opium, the Act also places controls on the importation, exportation and manufacture of tincture of cannabis and proparations containing dihydrocodeine. It also creates an offence of being an occupier of premises permitting the smoking of prepared opium (compare section 8 of the MDA) and introduces the offence of performing acts in this country resulting in the commission of an offence contrary to a corresponding law abroad (compare section 20 of the MDA).

Second Opium Conference and Geneva Convention 1925. Discusses cannabis as well as opium. Introduces independent body to monitor and advise on matters relating to opiate distribution and control. Also sets up a system of annual reporting of drug stocks, manufacture and shipments.

Dangerous Drugs Act 1925 amends 1920 Act so as to restrict importation and exportation of coca leaf and cannabis.

Report of the Interdepartmental Committee on Morphine and Heroin Addiction (the Rolleston Committee) 1926 recommends that prescription of heroin and morphine be permitted for the cure of addiction by gradual withdrawal and to incurable addicts.

International Convention for Limiting the Manufacture and Regulating the Distribution of Narcotic Drugs 1931 introduces requirement for countries to produce estimates of drug consumption and other statistics. Limits manufacture of narcotic drugs to medical and scientific purposes.

Dangerous Drugs Act 1932 extends range of controlled drugs following 1931 convention and prohibits trade in and manufacture of opium and cocaine for other than medical and scientific purposes.

Convention for the Suppression of Illicit Traffic in Dangerous Drugs 1936.

Geneva Protocol 1946 transfers functions of League of Nations, of which the United States was not a member, to the United Nations.

Dangerous Drugs (Amendment) Act 1950 enables United Kingdom legislation to reflect Geneva Protocol.

Paris Protocol 1948 authorises World Health Organisation to report on any substance capable of causing dependence and which might warrant international control.

Dangerous Drugs Act 1951 consolidates previous Dangerous Drugs Acts.

Opium Protocol (New York) 1953 starts process of consolidation of international agreements.

Single Convention on Narcotic Drugs 1961.

Report of the Interdepartmental Committee on Drug Addiction 1961 (the First Brain Committee) says further controls on heroin and cocaine not needed.

Dangerous Drugs Act 1964, passed to enable United Kingdom to ratify Single Convention, creates new offence of cultivation of cannabis.

Drugs (Prevention of Misuse) Act 1964 introduces controls over amphetamines including making their unlawful possession an offence.

Dangerous Drugs Act 1965 consolidates previous Dangerous Drugs Acts including the Dangerous Drugs Act 1964 but not the Drugs (Prevention of Misuse) Act 1964).

Second Report of the Interdepartmental Committee on Addiction (the second Brain report) recommends in 1965 the notification of addicts and that only licensed doctors be allowed to prescribe heroin and cocaine to addicts.

Drugs (Prevention of Misuse) Act Modification Order 1966 introduces controls over lysergic acid diethylamide (LSD) including making its unlawful possession an offence.

Dangerous Drugs Act 1967 implements recommendations of second Brain report and introduces national powers to stop and search people and vehicles for drugs.

Misuse of Drugs Act 1971.

The Convention on Psychotropic Substances 1971.

Intoxicating Substances (Supply) Act 1985 prohibits sale of substances to people under 18 if there is reason to believe that they will be inhaled or swallowed.

The Controlled Drugs (Penalties) Act 1985 increases the maximum penalty for trafficking offences to life imprisonment.

The Drug Trafficking Offences Act 1986 introduces measures to confiscate assets of drugs trade. Now largely replaced by Drug Trafficking Act 1994.

Convention Against Illicit Traffic in Narcotic and Psychotropic Substances 1988 (the Vienna Convention).

Part II of the Criminal Justice (International Co-operation) Act 1990 implements the Vienna Convention's requirements for regulating the manufacture and supply of precursors.

Drug Trafficking Act 1994.

Crime (Sentences) Act 1997 introduces mandatory minimum seven year sentences for people convicted for the third time of a drug trafficking offence involving a Class A drug.

Appendix 6

Associated Publications

The following documents were produced specifically in order to inform the work of the Inquiry. Although not at present published, they can be made available on request.

1   *Room for Manoeuvre. Overview of comparative legal research into national drug laws of France, Germany, Italy, Spain, the Netherlands and Sweden and their relation to three international drugs conventions.* Nicholas Dorn and Alison Jamieson, Institute for the Study of Drug Dependence. London 1999.

2   *Despite the Law. The Dynamics of Deciding to Use Illicit Drugs.* Professor Howard Parker, Manchester University. November 1998.

3   *Financial Measures against Illegal Drugs: An Overview.* Michael Levi, University of Cardiff. May 1999.

4   *Attitudes towards the law and drugs. Schools' Omnibus Survey.* MORI, London. April 1999.

5   *Attitudes towards the law and drugs. Adults' Omnibus Survey.* MORI, London. April 1999.

6   *Regulatory Drug Use.* Professor Robert Baldwin, London School of Economics and Political Science. January 1999.